The Role of Women in Making and Building Peace in Liberia

Gender Sensitivity versus Masculinity

Anne Theobald

THE ROLE OF WOMEN IN MAKING AND BUILDING PEACE IN LIBERIA

Gender Sensitivity versus Masculinity

ibidem-Verlag
Stuttgart

Bibliographic information published by the Deutsche Nationalbibliothek

Die Deutsche Nationalbibliothek lists this publication in the Deutsche Nationalbibliografie; detailed bibliographic data are available in the Internet at http://dnb.d-nb.de.

Bibliografische Information der Deutschen Nationalbibliothek

Die Deutsche Nationalbibliothek verzeichnet diese Publikation in der Deutschen Nationalbibliografie; detaillierte bibliografische Daten sind im Internet über http://dnb.d-nb.de abrufbar.

Cover picture: © olly - Fotolia.com

ISBN-13: 978-3-8382-0386-7

© *ibidem*-Verlag / *ibidem* Press

Stuttgart, Germany 2012

Printed in the United States of America

CONTENTS

List of Abbreviations

AFL	Armed Forces of Liberia
CPA	Comprehensive Peace Agreement
DDRR	Disarmament, Demobilisation, Rehabilitation, Reintegration
DFID	Department for International Development
ECOMOG	ECOWAS Ceasefire Monitoring Group
ECOWAS	Economic Community of West African States
FGM	Female genital mutilation
GTZ	Gesellschaft für Technische Zusammenarbeit (German technical cooperation)
HIV/AIDS	Human immunodeficiency virus/acquired immunodeficiency syndrome
IDP	Internally Displaced Person
INPFL	Independent National Patriotic Front of Liberia
LDF	Lofa Defense Force
LPC	Liberia Peace Council
LUDF	Liberian United Democratic Front
LURD	Liberians United for Reconciliation and Democracy
LWI	Liberian Women's Initiative
MARWOPNET	Mano River Union Women Peace Network
MODEL	Movement for Democracy in Liberia
NEC	National Elections Commission
NGO	Non-governmental organisation
NPFL	National Patriotic Front of Liberia
SALW	Small arms and light weapons
TRC	Truth and Reconciliation Commission
ULIMO	United Movement for Democracy in Liberia
ULIMO-J	United Liberation Movement of Liberia for Democracy-Johnson faction
ULIMO-K	United Liberation Movement of Liberia for Democracy-Kromah faction

UN	United Nations
UNMIL	United Nations Mission in Liberia
UNOMIL	United Nations Observer Mission in Liberia
UNSCR	United Nations Security Council Resolution
WANEP	West Africa Network for Peacebuilding
WIPNET	Women in Peacebuilding Network

1. Introduction[*]

In the early 2000s, Liberian women wearing wrap skirts, white T-shirts and shouting 'We want peace, no more war' attracted international attention: After almost fifteen years of civil strife (1989-2003), the enduring active, non-violent campaigning by women's organisations for peace that included various activities such as organising demonstrations, religious actions and negotiating with politicians and factional leaders, contributed to the ending of the fighting in the small West African country.[1] In 2005, Ellen Johnson-Sirleaf won the post-conflict elections and became the first female head of state elected by public vote in Africa.

[*] The author would like to thank Karen Abi-Ezzi, Donna Pankhurst, Fiona Macaulay and Mohammed Sajid for their fruitful comments and constructive criticism on earlier versions of this work.

[1] African Women and Peace Support Group. *Liberian Women Peacemakers: Fighting for the Right to Be Seen, Heard, and Counted*. Trenton, Africa World Press, 2004; Badmus, Alani. 'Explaining Women's Roles in the West African Tragic Triplet: Sierra Leone, Liberia, and Cote d'Ivoire in Comparative Perspective'. In: *Journal of Alternative Perspectives in the Social Sciences*, Vol. 1, No. 3, 2009, pp. 808-839; Barnes, Elisabeth. *Agents for Change: Civil Society Roles in Preventing War & Building Peace*. Den Haag, European Centre for Conflict Prevention, International Secretariat of the Global Partnership for the Prevention of Armed Conflict (Issue Paper 2), 2006. Available online at: http://www.gppac.net/documents/GPPAC/Research/Issue_papers_2006_-_2007_/2__ for_Change.pdf (Accessed on 02 May 2011), pp. 44-45; Ekiyor, Thelma Aremiebi & Gbowee, Leymah Roberta. *Women's Peace Activism in West Africa: The WIPNET Experience* [Website]. 2005. Available online at: http://www.peoplebuildingpeace.org/ thestories/article.php?id=80&typ=theme&pid=18 (Accessed on 27 April 2011); Fleshman, Michael. 'African Women Struggle for a Seat at the Peace Table'. In: *Africa Renewal* [Website], Vol., 16, No. 4, 2003. Available online at: http://www.un.org/ ecosocdev/geninfo/afrec/vol16no4/164wm1.htm (Accessed on 23 April 2011); George, Kla Emmanuel Gamoe. *Women as Agents of Peace During the Civil Wars in Liberia and Sierra Leone, 1989—2005*. Undated. (Mimeographed Paper). Available online at: www.isud.typepad.com/files/george1.doc (Accessed on 28 April 2011); Pedersen, Jennifer. 'In the Rain and in the Sun: Women in Peacebuilding in Liberia'. International Studies Association Annual Convention on *Bridging Multiple Divides*. San Francisco, 26-29 March 2008. Available online at: http://www.allacademic.com//meta/p_mla_ apa_research_citation/2/5/3/1/3/pages253135/p253135-1.php (Accessed on 25 April 2011); Solomon, Christiana. 'The Mano River Union Sub-region: The Role of Women in Building Peace'. In: Baksh, Rawwida et al. (eds.). *Gender Mainstreaming in Conflict Transformation: Building Sustainable Peace*. London, Commonwealth Secretariat, 2005, pp. 171-180.

1.1. Rationale and definition of key terms

Women's participation in peacemaking and peacebuilding in Liberia seems exceptional in two ways, which is why it was chosen as a country case study for this analysis. Firstly, Liberian women suffer from various forms of discrimination because of (patriarchal) socio-cultural structures and their consequences.[2] This is reflected on the individual, community and state level. Secondly, empirical findings show that females tend to be neglected or even totally absent in peace processes, particularly in official negotiations: Women make up an average of eight per cent of participants in peace negotiations, the percentage of female signatories of peace agreements only amounts to three per cent. In many peace processes, for example, in Somalia, Côte d'Ivoire, the Central African Republic, Nepal and Indonesia, women did not participate at all.[3]

The present study will consider women's participation with reference to three organisations – the Liberian Women's Initiative (LWI), the Mano River Union Women Peace Network (MARWOPNET) and the Women in Peacebuilding Network (WIPNET). They are particularly prominent because they comprised female members from different social, religious and ethnic backgrounds. Furthermore, not only did they engage in grassroots actions, e.g. marches or strikes, but they were also strongly active at a high political level by lobbying

---

[2] See Fleshman, Michael. op. cit.; Fuest, Veronika. 'This Is the Time to Go in Front': Changing Roles and Opportunities for Women in Liberia'. In: *African Affairs*, Vol. 107, No. 427, 2008, pp. 201–224; Richards, Paul. 'Young Men and Gender in War and Postwar Reconstruction: Some Comparative Findings from Liberia and Sierra Leone. In: Bannon, Ian & Correia, Maria C. (eds.). *The Other Half of Gender: Men's Issues in Development.* Washington D.C., The World Bank, 2006, pp. 195-218; United Nations Educational, Scientific and Cultural Organization (UNESCO) (ed.). *Women and Peace in Africa: Case Studies on Traditional Conflict Resolution Practices.* Paris, 2003, pp. 7-8. Available online at: http://unesdoc.unesco.org/images/0013/001332/133274e.pdf (Accessed on 02 May 2011).

[3] United Nations Development Fund for Women (UNIFEM). *Women's Participation in Peace Negotiations: Connections between Presence and Influence.* New York, 2009, pp. 1-2. Available online at: http://www.realizingrights.org/pdf/UNIFEM_handout_ Women_in_peace_processes_Brief_April_20_2009.pdf (Accessed on 25 August 2011); UNESCO. op. cit., p. 8; United Nations Women. *Women, War and Peace* [Website]. Undated. Available online at: http://www.womenwarpeace.org/ (Accesses on 25 August 2011); *Zanzibar Declaration: Women of Africa for a Culture of Peace.* 1999. Available online at: http://www.unesco.org/cpp/uk/declarations/zanzibar.htm (Accessed on 02 May 2011).

politicians and rebels as well as participating in negotiations and peace talks on a sub-regional level.[4] These are *peacemaking* activities, i.e. attempts to reach an agreement between warring factions to end violence and fighting. In addition to those, women supported disarmament and reintegration of ex-combatants and child soldiers and undertook measures to overcome the underlying root causes of violent conflict and promote reconciliation over the longer term. These are *peacebuilding* activities, which aim at overcoming structural reasons of conflict, reconciling divided societies and preventing future conflict in the long run.[5] In the following, both peacemaking and peacebuilding in Liberia are considered as part of the Liberian *peace process*.

This analysis will focus on internal peacemaking and peacebuilding efforts by women's organisations. International political influence is not systematically taken into account in order to assess impact and scope of women's political activities in an un-distorted and independent way.[6]

Political activities of women's groups during the entire conflict period (1989-2003) are analysed. Terminologically, this period is referred to as *Liberian conflict or conflicts*, because the two civil wars, which lasted from 1989 to 1997 and from 1999 to 2003, respectively, are strongly intertwined.[7] If the author only refers to one of the civil wars, she will speak of the *first* or *second* one.

---

[4] The West African sub-region is understood politically and refers to the members of the Economic Community of West African States (ECOWAS).

[5] Detailed definitions of the terms *peacemaking* and *peacebuilding* are given in chapter 2.1. For more information, see also Ettang, Dorcas; Maina, Grace & Razia, Warigia. *A Regional Approach to Peacebuilding – The Mano River Region.* Durban, African Centre for the Constructive Resolution of Disputes (ACCORD), Policy and Practice Brief Issue 6 (May), 2011, pp. 1-2. Available online at: http://www.accord.org.za/downloads/brief/policy_practice6.pdf (Accessed on 17 August 2011); Jones, Katelyn. 'West African Women Unite: The Inclusion of Women in Peace Processes'. In: *Undergraduate Transitional Justice Review*, Vol. 1, No. 2, 2011, p. 156; Ramsbotham, Oliver; Woodhouse, Tom & Miall, Hugh. *Contemporary Conflict Resolution: The Prevention, Management and Transformation of Deadly Conflicts.* Cambridge, Polity Press, 2005, p. 30.

[6] The international community, especially the United Nations, played a considerable role in the post-conflict reconstruction. Its influence is assessed and integrated into the analysis when this is relevant. United Nations. *UNMIL: United Nations Mission in Liberia* [Website]. Undated. Available online at: http://www.un.org/en/peacekeeping/missions/unmil/mandate.shtml (Accessed on 18 August 2011).

[7] Reisinger, Christian. 'A Framework for the Analysis of Post-conflict Situations: Liberia and Mozambique Reconsidered. In: *International Peacekeeping*, Vol. 16, No. 4, 2009, p. 488.

In the field of conflict transformation and development policy, women's inclusion into peace processes is advocated because it is assumed to lead to so-called gender-sensitive post-conflict orders.[8] Gender sensitivity is

> "[t]he ability to recognize gender issues and especially the ability to recognize women's different perceptions and interests arising from their different social location and different gender roles."[9]

These perceptions and interests then have to be integrated into policies, such as disarmament, demobilisation, rehabilitation and reintegration (DDRR) or reforms of the justice and security sectors. Therefore, one can define gender sensitive peace as a state, where the specific requirements of both genders have been integrated into policies and measures. As a consequence, gendered aspects of conflicts, i.e. factors discriminating against women (or men), direct (physical, institutional, sexual, political, cultural or economic) and structural violence are overcome in the public and the private sphere.[10] Gender

---

[8] Derbyshire, Helen. *Gender Manual: A Practical Guide for Development Policy Makers and Practitioners.* London, Department for International Development, 2002. Available online at: http://www.allindiary.org/pool/resources/dfid-gender-manual.pdf (Accessed on 11 May 2011); Gesellschaft für technische Zusammenarbeit (GTZ). *Towards Gender Mainstreaming in Crisis Prevention and Conflict Management: Guidelines for the German Technical Cooperation.* Eschborn, 2001; United Nations Women. op. cit., *Women, War and Peace*; United Nations Security Council (UNSC). *Resolution 1325 (2000).* New York, 2000. Available online at: http://www.un.org/events/res_1325.pdf (Accessed on 27 October 2010); United Nations Security Council (UNSC). *Resolution 1820 (2008).* New York, 2008. Available online at: http://daccess-dds-ny.un.org/doc/UNDOC/GEN/N08/391/44/PDF/N0839144.pdf?OpenElement (Accessed on 25 August 2011).

[9] United States Agency for International Development (USAID). *Gender Terminology.* Undated, p. 3. Available online at: http://www.usaid.gov/our_work/cross-cutting_programs/wid/pubs/Gender_Terminology_2.pdf (Accessed on 18 August 2011).

[10] Funder, Maria. 'Die Konflikttheorie feministischer Theorien'. In: Bonacker, Thorsten (ed.) *Sozialwissenschaftliche Konflikttheorien: Eine Einführung.* Wiesbaden, VS Verlag für Wissenschaften, 2008, pp. 297-299; Kreile, Renate. 'Dame, Bube, König... – Das neue große Spiel um Afghanistan und der Gender-Faktor'. In: *Leviathan*, Vol. 30, No. 1, 2002, p. 37; Pankhurst, Donna. 'Introduction: Gendered War and Peace'. In: ibid. (ed.). *Gendered Peace: Women's Struggles for Post-War Justice and Reconciliation.* London, Routledge, 2008, pp. 5-6; Pankhurst, Donna. 'Post-War Backlash Violence against Women: What Can "Masculinity" Explain?' In: ibid. (ed.). *Gendered Peace: Women's Struggles for Post-War Justice and Reconciliation.* London, Routledge, 2008, p. 293; Ramsbotham, Oliver; Woodhouse, Tom & Miall, Hugh. op. cit., pp. 265-274; Zalewski, Marysia. 'Feminist International Relations: Making Sense...' In: Shepherd, Laura J. (ed.). *Gender Matters in Global Politics. A Feminist Introduction to International Relations.* Abingdon, Routledge, 2010, pp. 29, 35-36.

sensitivity is not conceptualised as an absolute, but as a relative measure that is seen against the particular background and situation of a country.

Surprisingly, despite women's participation in peacemaking and peacebuilding in Liberia, there seem to be few improvements in terms of gender sensitivity after the conflict (for example, adjustments of laws in favour of women) compared to the marginalisation, discrimination and even violence women continue to face.[11] Therefore, the study will not only focus on women's commitment for peace, but look beyond it by assessing actual outcomes and consequences of their political activities.

A potentially adverse influence in this regard is masculinity, meaning the way manhood is constructed within a society – the male "gender identity".[12] This seems relevant in the context of conflict because, firstly, patterns of masculinity permeate organisational and political structures such as the state.[13] Secondly, there are interactions between certain features of masculine identities and the emergence and increase of violence against women in the aftermath

---

[11] For more information, see section 5.1. or Badmus, Alani. op. cit.; George, Kla Emmanuel Gamoe. op. cit., Kellow, Tim. *Women, Elections and Violence in West Africa: Assessing Women's Political Participation in Liberia and Sierra Leone.* London, International Alert, 2010. Available online at: http://www.international-alert.org/sites/default/ files/publications/201012WomenElectionsViolenceWestAfrica.pdf (Accessed on 20 July 2011); Truth and Reconciliation Commission of Liberia. *"Inheritance Law Not Protecting Women"... Attorney Deweh Gray* [Website]. Press Releases. Undated. Available online at: http://trcofliberia.org/press_releases/109 (Accessed on 21 July 2011); United Nations Development Programme (UNDP). *Liberia: Country Profile of Human Development Indicators* [Website]. New York, 2011. Available online at: http://hdrstats. undp.org/en/countries/profiles/LBR.html (Accessed on 18 June 2011); United Nations General Assembly. *Liberia Is Writing New History for Its Women and Girls Delegation Tells Women's Anti-Discrimination Committee, Admitting Great Challenges in That Endeavour* [Website]. New York, 2009. Available online at: http://www.un.org/News/ Press/docs/2009/wom1748.doc.htm (Accessed on 20 July 2011).

[12] Goldstein, Joshua S. *War and Gender.* Cambridge, Cambridge University Press, 2001, p. 251.

[13] Connell, Raewyn W. *The Men and the Boys.* Cambridge, Polity Press, 2000, pp. 11, 213, 215-217; 220-223; Connell, Raewyn W. *Gender.* Cambridge, Polity Press, 2002, pp. 102-104; Connell, Raewyn W. *Masculinities.* Cambridge, Polity Press, 2005, pp. xx-xxi, 72-73; Enloe, Cynthia. *Bananas, Beaches and Bases: Making Feminist Sense of International Politics.* Berkeley, University of California Press, 1989, pp. 10, 195-196; Hearn, Jeff. 'Violence, Organisational and Collective'. In: Flood, Michael et al. *International Encyclopedia of Men and Masculinities.* London, Routledge, 2007, p. 619; Higate, Paul. 'Military Institutions'. In: Flood, Michael et al. *International Encyclopedia of Men and Masculinities.* London, Routledge, 2007, p. 441.

of conflicts.[14] This work will examine interactions and counteractions between and against women in the making and building of peace; gender sensitivity; and masculinity.

1.2. Research questions

The primary research question of the study at hand is: *To what extent has the role of women in the Liberian peacemaking and peacebuilding contributed to gender-sensitive outcomes in post-conflict Liberian society?* Other secondary research question are: In *qualitative and quantitative terms, to what extent have peace-building activities led to a gender-sensitive peace at the micro, mezzo and macro level of post-conflict Liberian society? And in what ways have the public and private manifestations of masculinity impacted Liberian women's attempts to construct a gender-sensitive peace?*
Qualitative factors refer to non-quantifiable domains and developments such as traditional perceptions of gender and include policies regarding gender issues and outcomes of policies. *Quantitative factors* subsume figures and proportions, for example the percentage of female members of parliament.

1.3. Methodology

Methodologically, a single case study approach is employed,[15] where Liberia has been chosen as the country case. The case study aims at "elaborating or expanding [the existing] body of theory with the resulting data".[16] The advantage of the selection of one case is that it can be analysed very profound-

---

[14] Alsop, Rachel; Fitzsimons, Annette & Lennon, Kathleen. *Theorizing Gender.* Cambridge, Polity Press, 2002, pp. 134-135; Connell, Raewyn W. op. cit., *The Men and the Boys*, pp. 20-21, 217, 224; Connell, Raewyn W. op. cit., *Masculinities*, pp. 82-84; Goldstein, Joshua S. op. cit., pp. 290-291, 293; Pankhurst, Donna. op. cit., 'Post-War Backlash Violence against Women', pp. 295-304; Pringle, Keith. 'Violence'. In: Flood, Michael et al. (eds.) *International Encyclopedia of Men and Masculinities.* London, Routledge, 2007, pp. 612-615; Whitehead, Stephen M. 'Patriarchal Dividend'. In: Flood, Michael et al. (eds.). *International Encyclopedia of Men and Masculinities.* London, Routledge, 2007, pp. 467-468. See also section 2.2.

[15] Peters, B. Guy. *Comparative Politics: Theory and Methods.* London, Macmillan Press, 1998, p. 62.

[16] ibid., p. 62; see also ibid., pp. 61-65.

ly. At the same time, it is assumed that the analysis of the study is applicable to other similar countries and hence highly relevant beyond the case examined.[17] The example chosen is a 'deviant' case. A so-called deviant case does not conform to assumptions based on an existing theory. In the Liberian example, one would expect that because of the suppositions mentioned above and because of women's participation in the Liberian peace process as well as the election of a female president, women's needs and interests were broadly taken into account in the post-conflict period. However, statistic and qualitative indicators show they were not.[18]

Within the country case study, the contribution of women's organisations is analysed by reference to three organisations chosen as examples. Here, internal difficulties that are connected to the procedure of the organisations and that impact on the degree of gender sensitivity are particularly considered. Subsequently, an analytical framework is applied to assess positive and negative developments in terms of gender sensitivity in post-conflict Liberia (see Appendix II). It is grounded in a combination of theoretical and policy-orientated literature as well as conflict analysis frameworks that reflect what is desirable to create a gender-sensitive peace.[19] It focuses on substantive fac-

---

[17] Landman, Todd. *Issues and Methods in Comparative Politics: An Introduction.* London, Routledge, 2003, p. 34.

[18] For more qualitative and quantitative information on the situation of women in Liberia, see section 5.1., Appendix III. or Aisha, Fatoumata. op. cit., Organisation for Economic Co-operation and Development – Social Institutions and Gender Index (OECD-SIGI). *Gender Equality and Social Institutions in Liberia* [Website]. 2011. Available online at: http://www.genderindex.org/country/Liberia (Accessed on 21 July 2011); United Nations Development Programme (UNDP). *Liberia Annual Report 2009.* Monrovia, 2009. Available online at: http://www.lr.undp.org/Documents/RecentPublic/UNDP%20Liberia%20Annual%20Report%202009.pdf (Accessed on 18 June 2011); UNDP. op. cit., *Liberia: Country*; United Nations General Assembly. *Liberia Is Writing New History for Its Women and Girls Delegation Tells Women's Anti-Discrimination Committee, Admitting Great Challenges in That Endeavour* [Website]. New York, 2009. Available online at: http://www.un.org/News/Press/docs/2009/wom1748.doc.htm (Accessed on 20 July 2011).

[19] See for example, Baksh, Rawwida. 'Gender Mainstreaming in Post-conflict Reconstruction'. In: Baksh, Rawwida et al. (eds.). *Gender Mainstreaming in Conflict Transformation: Building Sustainable Peace.* London, Commonwealth Secretariat, 2005, pp. 82-98; Department for International Development (DFID). *Conducting Conflict Assessments: Guidance Notes.* London, 2002, pp. 10, 12, 27-33. Available online at: http://webarchive.nationalarchives.gov.uk/+/http://www.dfid.gov.uk/documents/publications/conflictassessmentguidance.pdf (Accessed on 27 June 2011); GTZ. op. cit., *To-*

tors in various domains, more precisely the political, security, legal, socio-economic and socio-cultural. External, i.e. sub-regional or international impacts are included only if relevant. The different spheres are examined by means of a multi-level analysis. This approach simultaneously considers relatively small contexts on the micro level (individual, family), the intermediary scale thanks to the mezzo level (community) and a large-scale perspective, the macro level (state, system) (see Appendix III).[20] Developments on different levels of analysis are disaggregated and examined. Interdependences between factors can be identified, which leads to a more encompassing understanding of dynamics. Hence, the manifold challenges and achievements that the Liberian post-war society faces in terms of gender sensitivity as well as relations between them become clearly visible and can be balanced against each other. In addition, the analysis considers long and short term, i.e. structural and directly conflict-related explanations.

In terms of sources, the study is a library-based research project. It relies on theoretical literature and secondary data in various languages. This data is taken from a variety of sources such as books, monographs, academic journal articles, reports by non-governmental and international organisations, websites relating to the armed conflict and peacebuilding in Liberia, as well as newspaper articles of different European, US-American and African media. Relevant primary sources including the Liberian constitution, peace agreements, declarations, laws, UN publications (e.g. resolutions) and speeches

---

wards *Gender Mainstreaming*; Gesellschaft für technische Zusammenarbeit (GTZ). *Conflict Analysis for Project Planning and Management: A Practical Guideline - Draft.* Eschborn, 2001, pp. 21, 76. Available online at: http://www.gtz.de/de/dokumente/en-crisis-conflictanalysis-2001.pdf (Accessed on 27 June 2011); United Nations Development Fund for Women (UNIFEM). *Securing the Peace: Guiding the International Community towards Women's Effective Participation throughout Peace Processes.* New York, 2005. Available online at: http://www.unifem.org/attachments/products/Securing _the_Peace.pdf (Accessed on 09 May 2011); Zuckerman, Elaine & Greenberg, Marcia. 'The Gender Dimensions of Post-Conflict Reconstruction: An Analytical Framework for Policymakers'. In: Sweetman, Caroline (ed.). *Gender, Peacebuilding and Reconstruction.* Oxford, Oxfam GB, 2005, pp. 70-82.

[20] See Landman, Todd. op. cit., p. 18; Nohlen, Dieter. 'Mikro-Makro-Analyse'. In: Nohlen, Dieter & Schultze, Rainer-Olaf (eds.). *Lexikon der Politikwissenschaft: Theorien, Methoden, Begriffe: Band 1.* München, Verlag C.H. Beck, 2004, p. 550; Schultze, Rainer-Olaf. 'Mehrebenen-Analyse'. In: Nohlen, Dieter & Schultze, Rainer-Olaf (eds.). *Lexikon der Politikwissenschaft: Theorien, Methoden, Begriffe: Band 1.* München, Verlag C.H. Beck, 2004, p. 528.

will complete the analysis. The material is carefully selected and assessed in order to ensure the objectivity, reliability and validity of the results.

1.4. Contribution to literature

This case study of Liberia contributes to a profound reflection and understanding of gender in (post-)conflict situations in Sub-Saharan Africa. It helps to refine and expand theories on peacemaking and peacebuilding by bringing together scholarly interpretations of the intersection between women, gender sensitivity and (dominant) masculinity at the micro, mezzo and macro level of post-conflict Liberian society.[21]

1.5. Structure

The structure is as follows. First of all, the theoretical framework of the field of gender, masculinity and issues of peace and conflict is presented. This chapter will discuss the relevance of gender in the context of peacemaking and peacebuilding from a theoretical viewpoint, introduce a theoretical approach to the significance of masculinity/masculinities and review literature on the connection of gender and peacemaking, peacebuilding and the impact of masculinity. The second chapter focuses on the socio-cultural and historical background of Liberia as well as its gender order and analyses reasons and the progression of the civil war. The third chapter deals with the role of women in conflict and the creation of peace and has a closer look at internal and procedural difficulties of women's movements relating to the latter. In the fourth chapter, Ellen Johnson-Sirleaf's electoral victory as well as her work during her first term of office is examined. The final chapter evaluates the quality of the post-conflict social order in terms of gender sensitivity and asks what factors influenced its development? Finally, theoretical conclusions from the findings are drawn.

---

[21] Gerring, John. *Case Study Research: Principles and Practices*. Cambridge, Cambridge University Press, 2003, pp. 105-106; Klotz, Audie, 'Case Selection'. In: Klotz, Audie & Prakash, Deepa (eds.). *Qualitative Methods in International Relations: A Pluralist Guide*. Basingstoke, Palgrave Macmillan, 2009, pp. 43-58; Landman, Todd. op. cit.

2. Theoretical approaches to gender and masculinity relating to issues of peace and conflict

This chapter introduces the key concepts at the basis of the analysis. Firstly, the importance of gender and gender sensitivity in relation to peace and conflict are discussed. Afterwards, the significance of masculinity is examined. Finally, the literature on gender in peacemaking and peacebuilding and the influence of masculinity in post-conflict settings is reviewed.

2.1. The importance of gender and gender sensitivity for the creation of peace and post-conflict orders

It is claimed that it is imperative to better include a gender perspective in conventional peacemaking and peacebuilding.[1] This does not mean that women are simply 'added' to existing notions, but these notions must be reconceptualised and extended. Therefore, one first has to define gender and gender sensitivity in order to develop a gender-sensitive notion of peace. Finally, the correlation between gender, peacemaking and peacebuilding will be critically evaluated.

Gender is a "socio-cultural construction"[2] that is created by different discursive practices, social differences and processes as well as history. Thus, it is formed by both structure and agency and should not be understood as existing naturally, biologically or universally.[3]

---

[1] Ramsbotham, Oliver; Woodhouse, Tom & Miall, Hugh. *Contemporary Conflict Resolution: The Prevention, Management and Transformation of Deadly Conflicts*. Cambridge, Polity Press, 2005, pp. 265-274; United Nations Security Council (UNSC). *Resolution 1325 (2000)*. New York, 2000. Available online at: http://www.un.org/events/ res_1325e.pdf (Accessed on 27 October 2010); Väyrynen, Tarja. 'Gender and Peacebuilding'. In: Richmond, Oliver P. (ed.) *Palgrave Advances in Peacebuilding: Critical Developments and Approaches*. Basingstoke, Palgrave Macmillan, 2010, pp. 137-153.

[2] Funder, Maria. 'Die Konflikttheorie feministischer Theorien'. In: Bonacker, Thorsten (ed.). *Sozialwissenschaftliche Konflikttheorien. Eine Einführung*. Wiesbaden, Verlag für Sozialwissenschaften, 2008, p. 294; translation by the author.

[3] Badmus, Alani. 'Explaining Women's Roles in the West African Tragic Triplet: Sierra Leone, Liberia, and Cote d'Ivoire in Comparative Perspective'. In: *Journal of Alternative*

11

Consequently, the way gender is perceived is contextually specific and varies in time, space and culture. Gender theory does not only focus on women's issues and aspects of femininity, but it also considers men, masculinity and interactions between women and men. Moser and Clark note that

> "[t]he differentiation between and relative positioning of women and men is seen as an important ordering principle that pervades the system of power and is sometimes its very embodiment."[4]

Hence, gender functions as a structural category that organises the lives of both women and men in all relevant societal domains (e.g. the "social, economic [and] political").[5] Not only do these – often asymmetric – power dynamics and relations influence the individual, but they also strongly impact on the societal, institutional, national or even international level.[6]

Due to their differing societal positions, the experiences, interests and needs of women and men vary. This is not always obvious and requires gender sensitivity, which is

> "[t]he ability to recognize gender issues and especially the ability to recognize women's different perceptions and interests arising from their different social location and different gender roles."[7]

Perspectives in the Social Sciences, Vol. 1, No. 3, 2009, pp. 810-811; Cockburn, Cynthia. 'The Gendered Dynamics of Armed Conflict and Political Violence'. In: Moser, Caroline O. N. & Clark, Fiona C. (eds.) _Victims, Perpetrators or Actors? Gender, Armed Conflict and Political Violence_. London, Zed Books, 2001, pp. 13-14, 16; Connell, Raewyn W. _Masculinities_. Cambridge, Polity Press, 2005, pp. 71-73, 81; El-Bushra, Judy. 'Transforming Conflict: Some Thoughts on a Gendered Understanding of Conflict Processes'. In: Jacobs, Susie, Jacobson, Ruth & Marchbank, Jennifer (eds.). _States of Conflict: Gender, Violence and Resistance_. London, Zed Books, 2000, pp. 66-67; Enloe, Cynthia. _Bananas, Beaches and Bases: Making Feminist Sense of International Politics_. Berkeley, University of California Press, 1989, p. 3; Funder, Maria. op. cit., pp. 294-295, 303; Giles, Wenona & Hyndman, Jennifer. 'Introduction: Gender and Conflict in a Global Context'. In: ibid. (eds.) _Sites of Violence: Gender and Conflict Zones_. London, University of California Press, 2004, p. 8; Moser, Caroline O. N. & Clark, Fiona C. 'Introduction'. In: ibid. (eds.). _Victims, Perpetrators or Actors? Gender, Armed Conflict and Political Violence_. London, Zed Books, 2001, pp. 3, 5.

[4] Cockburn, Cynthia. op. cit., 'The Gendered Dynamics of Armed Conflict and Political Violence', p. 15.

[5] ibid., p. 15.

[6] ibid., pp. 24-25; El-Bushra, Judy. op. cit., p. 76; Enloe, Cynthia. op. cit., p. 3; Funder, Maria. op. cit., p. 293; Moser, Caroline O. N. & Clark, Fiona C. op. cit., p. 5.

[7] United States Agency for International Development (USAID). _Gender Terminology_. Undated, p. 3. Available online at: http://www.usaid.gov/our_work/cross-cutting_ programs/wid/pubs/Gender_Terminology_2.pdf (Accessed on 18 August 2011).

12

Gender sensitivity does not draw a picture where women and men confront each other. It is the first step towards gender awareness, equality or equity.[8] However, other than these, gender sensitivity is a more neutral term aiming at the identification of differences, not at radical changes.[9]

Following on from this, the terms peacemaking and peacebuilding will be clarified. Peacemaking refers to the immediate attempt of creating peace by "moving towards settlement of armed conflict, where conflict parties are induced to reach agreement voluntarily".[10] It focuses on the short-term, i.e. the cessation of violence, and comprises non-violent measures to compromise and stop fighting.[11] In Liberia, peacemaking – specifically negotiations, peace talks and mediation – was supported by the Economic Community of West African States (ECOWAS), while women's organisations exerted a certain, although sometimes unofficial influence, too. In contrast to this, peacebuilding deals with structural, underlying contradictions and causes of conflict on a long-term basis.[12] It complements peacemaking by seeking to

"prevent, reduce, transform and help people recover from structural and other forms of violence [and] to break cycles of violence."[13]

Hence, the objective of peacebuilding is to establish sustainable peace and prevent future conflicts.[14] This includes various activities on different levels,

---

[8] For a definition of these, see ibid., pp. 2-3.

[9] Cockburn, Cynthia. op. cit., 'The Gendered Dynamics of Armed Conflict and Political Violence', p. 28; USAID. op. cit., *Gender Terminology*, p. 3.

[10] Ramsbotham, Oliver; Woodhouse, Tom & Miall, Hugh. op. cit., p. 30. See also Boutros-Ghali, Boutros. *An Agenda for Peace: Preventive Diplomacy, Peacemaking and Peacekeeping* [Website]. New York, United Nations, 1992. Available online at: http://www.un.org/Docs/SG/agpeace.html (Accessed on 18 August 2011), Cockburn, Cynthia. 'The Continuum of Violence: A Gender Perspective on War and Peace'. In: Giles, Wenona & Hyndman, Jennifer (eds.). *Sites of Violence: Gender and Conflict Zones*. London, University of California Press, 2004, p. 37

[11] United Nations (UN). *Charter of the United Nations and Statute of the International Court of Justice*. San Francisco, 1945, chapter VI. Available online at: http://treaties.un.org/doc/Publication/CTC/uncharter.pdf (Accessed on 18 August 2011).

[12] Cockburn, Cynthia. op. cit., 'The Continuum of Violence', p. 37; Ettang, Dorcas; Maina, Grace & Razia, Warigia. *A Regional Approach to Peacebuilding – The Mano River Region*. Durban, African Centre for the Constructive Resolution of Disputes (ACCORD), Policy and Practice Brief Issue 6 (May), 2011, p. 2. Available online at: http://www.accord.org.za/downloads/brief/policy_practice6.pdf (Accessed on 17 August 2011); Ramsbotham, Oliver; Woodhouse, Tom & Miall, Hugh. op. cit., p. 30.

[13] Ettang, Dorcas; Maina, Grace & Razia, Warigia. op. cit., p. 1.

for example disarmament, reintegration of ex-combatants and refugees, building and reforming of institutions or promotion of development, political participation and human rights.[15] In the context of the present study, peacebuilding is not understood as a predominantly external endeavour inspired by liberalism, as is often the case.[16]

As the quality of post-conflict Liberian society will be examined in terms of its gender sensitivity, a gender-sensitive definition of peace has to be developed. According to Galtung, positive peace is more than the absence of direct (e.g. physical, institutional, sexual, political, cultural or economic) violence, but includes "the integration of human society",[17] whereas structural violence must be overcome, too. Structural violence exists "when human beings are being influenced so that their actual somatic and mental realisations are below their potential realisation".[18] This understanding must be further broadened in order to be gender-sensitive. Here, definitions of Carolyn Nordstrom and Cynthia Cockburn are useful in order to capture various violent dynamics in different settings. Nordstrom's defines conflict

---

[14] ibid., p. 1; Jones, Katelyn. 'West African Women Unite: The Inclusion of Women in Peace Processes'. In: *Undergraduate Transitional Justice Review*, Vol. 1, No. 2, 2011, p. 156; Ramsbotham, Oliver; Woodhouse, Tom & Miall, Hugh. op. cit., p. 30.

[15] Boutros-Ghali, Boutros. op. cit., David, Charles-Philippe. 'Does Peacebuilding Build Peace? Liberal (Mis)steps in the Peace Process.' In: *Security Dialogue*, Vol. 30, No. 1, 1999; Ettang, Dorcas; Maina, Grace & Razia, Warigia. op. cit., p. 2.

[16] See, for example, David, Charles-Philippe. op. cit.; Väyrynen, Tarja. op. cit., pp. 139-140.

[17] Galtung, Johan. 'An Editorial'. In: *Journal of Peace Research*, Vol. 1, No. 1, 1964, p. 2. In contrast to this, negative peace is understood as "absence of violence, absence of war." Ibid., p. 2

[18] Galtung, Johan as quoted in Grewal, Baljit Singh. *Johan Galtung: Positive and Negative Peace*. Auckland, 2003, p. 2. Available online at: http://www.activeforpeace.org/no/fred/Positive_Negative_Peace.pdf (Accessed on 15 June 2011). See also Grewal, Baljit Singh. op. cit., pp. 2-3; Harders, Cilja. 'Krieg und Frieden in internationalen Beziehungen'. In: Rosenberger, Sieglinde & Sauer, Birgit (eds.). *Politikwissenschaft und Geschlecht. Konzepte – Verknüpfungen – Perspektiven*. Wien, Facultas Verlag, 2004, p. 235; Pillay, Anu. 'Violence against Women in the Aftermath'. In: Meintjes, Sheila; Pillay, Anu & Turshen, Meredeth (eds.). *The Aftermath: Women in Post-Conflict Transformation*. London, Zed Books, 2001, p. 37.

"[n]ot as a locale but as a process; not as distinct sets of troops, but as a compendium of international actors and forces visible, ethnographically, at any site of inquiry".[19]

Moreover, Cynthia Cockburn's notion of a "gendered continuum of violence"[20] refers to the difficulty to clearly distinguish between the pre-war and the post-war period, as domestic, gendered and sexual violence persist and even increase after armed conflicts, which means that women do not necessarily live in peace after an agreement was signed and fighting ended.[21] These feminist perspectives emphasise that violence is not restricted to conflict situations, war fronts or the public sphere, but it is private, pervading and ubiquitous in terms of time and space, strongly affecting the lives of women and other disempowered sections of the population.[22] Therefore, peace can only be gender-sensitive if it overcomes all forms of (gender-based) violence in the public and the private sphere,[23] in the political, economic and social domain and at the individual, sub-state and state level.[24]

---

[19] Nordstrom, Carolyn. 'Visible Wars and Invisible Girls, Shadow Industries, and the Politics of Not-Knowing'. In: *International Feminist Journal of Politics*, Vol. 1, No. 1, 1999, p. 21. See also Waylen, Georgina. *Gender in Third World Politics*. Buckingham, Open University Press, 1996, pp. 2-3.

[20] Cockburn, Cynthia. op. cit., 'The Continuum of Violence', p. 43.

[21] Pankhurst, Donna. 'Introduction: Gendered War and Peace'. In: ibid. (ed.). *Gendered Peace: Women's Struggles for Post-War Justice and Reconciliation*. London, Routledge, 2008, pp. 5-6; Pankhurst, Donna. 'Post-War Backlash Violence against Women: What Can "Masculinity" Explain?' In: ibid. (ed.). *Gendered Peace: Women's Struggles for Post-War Justice and Reconciliation*. London, Routledge, 2008, p. 293.

[22] Enloe, Cynthia. op. cit., pp. 195, 197; Harders, Cilja. op. cit., p. 243; Nordstrom, Carolyn. op. cit., p. 16; Waylen, Georgina. op. cit., pp. 2-3.

[23] Gender-based violence "encompasses a range of acts of violence committed against females because they are females and against males because they are males, based on how a particular society assigns and views roles and expectations for these people. It includes sexual violence, intimate partner or spouse abuse (domestic violence), emotional and psychological abuse, sex trafficking, forced prostitution, sexual exploitation, sexual harassment, harmful traditional practices (e.g., FGM, forced marriage, infanticide of girl children), and discriminatory practices based on gender." Vann, Beth. *Gender-Based Violence: Emerging Issues in Programs Serving Displaced Populations*. Arlington, Reproductive Health for Refugees Consortium, 2002, p. 8. Available online at: http://reliefweb.int/sites/reliefweb.int/files/resources/DA3C3605C463011DC1256D2D00 5A99E2-rhrc-GBV-jan03.pdf (Accessed on 29 August 2011).

[24] Funder, Maria. op. cit., pp. 297-299; Kreile, Renate. 'Dame, Bube, König... – Das neue große Spiel um Afghanistan und der Gender-Faktor'. In: *Leviathan*, Vol. 30, No. 1, 2002, p. 37; Ramsbotham, Oliver; Woodhouse, Tom & Miall, Hugh. op. cit., pp. 265-274; Zalewski, Marysia. 'Feminist International Relations: Making Sense...' In: Shepherd, Laura J. (ed.). *Gender Matters in Global Politics. A Feminist Introduction to International Relations*. Abingdon, Routledge, 2010, pp. 29, 35-36.

The idea of gender sensitivity is highly relevant in the context of peace processes.[25] Women are often marginalised or even discriminated against in peacemaking and peacebuilding.[26] They are, among others, quantitatively underrepresented at the decision-making level, including peace talks, and their specific perspectives, needs and interests relating to (post-)conflict situations are neglected in relation to policies.[27] Hence, academics claimed that gender aspects should be included into both short-term and long-term efforts to create peace as well as into post-conflict reconstruction.[28] This is supposed to lead to a more sustainable, just and inclusive peace, as the position of a social group that tends to be marginalised will finally be taken into account.[29]

[25] Bouta, Tsjeard et al. *Gender, Conflict, and Development*. Washington D.C., The World Bank, 2005, pp. 51-52.

[26] ibid., p. 51; 'Gender and Peacebuilding'. Background Paper prepared for Working Group 12, organized by Cordaid and Pax Christi (the Netherlands) and International Alert (UK), for the International Conference *Towards Better Peacebuilding Practice*, October 24-26, 2001, Soesterberg, the Netherlands. In: Galama, Anneke & Tongeren, Paul van (eds.). *Towards Better Peacebuilding Practice: On Lessons Learned, Evaluation Practices and Aid and Conflict*. Utrecht, European Centre for Conflict Prevention, 2003, p. 224; United Nations Women. *Women, War and Peace* [Website]. Undated. Available online at: http://www.womenwarpeace.org/ (Accessed on 25 August 2011); Väyrynen, Tarja. op. cit., pp. 143-144.

[27] Cockburn, Cynthia. op. cit., 'The Continuum of Violence', pp. 28-30; Connell, Raewyn W. op. cit., *Masculinities*, p. 73; Dittmer, Cordula. *Gender, Konflikt, Konfliktbearbeitung. Zivile und militärische Ansätze, Forderungen und Probleme*. Marburg (CCS Working Papers, No. 6), 2007, p. 4. Available online at: http://www.uni-marburg.de/konflikt forschung/pdf/ccswp06 (Accessed on 28 April 2011); Enloe, Cynthia. op. cit., p. 1; Gierycz, Dorota. 'Women, Peace and the United Nations'. Beyond Beijing'. In: Skjelsbæk, Inger & Smith, Dan (eds.). *Gender, Peace and Conflict*. Oslo, International Peace Research Institute, 2001, pp. 15, 21-23; Goldstein, Joshua S. *War and Gender*. Cambridge, Cambridge University Press, 2001, pp. 35-38; Harders, Cilja, op, cit., pp. 230-231; Jones, Adam. 'Does 'Gender' Make the World Go Round? Feminist Critiques of International Relations'. In: *Review of International Studies*, No. 22, 1996, p. 405, 408, 412; Mordt, Gabriele. 'Das Geschlechterarrangement der klassischen Sicherheitspolitik'. In: Harders, Cilja & Roß, Bettina (eds.). *Geschlechterverhältnisse in Krieg und Frieden: Perspektiven der feministischen Analyse internationaler* Beziehungen. Opladen, Leske & Budrich, 2002, p. 62; Moser, Caroline O. N. & Clark, Fiona C. op. cit., p. 4; Shepherd, Laura J. 'Sex or Gender? Bodies in World Politics and Why Gender Matters'. In: ibid. (ed.). *Gender Matters in Global Politics. A Feminist Introduction to International Relations*. Abingdon, Routledge, 2010, p. 5; Steans, Jill. *Gender and International Relations: An Introduction*. Cambridge, Polity Press, 1998, op. cit., p. 1; Zalewski, Marysia, op. cit., pp. 31, 37.

[28] Bouta, Tsjeard et al. op. cit., pp. 2, 51-52; Pankhurst, Donna. op cit., 'Introduction', pp. 25-26. See also Ramsbotham, Oliver; Woodhouse, Tom & Miall, Hugh. op. cit., pp. 265-274; Väyrynen, Tarja. op. cit., pp. 137-153.

[29] Dittmer, Cordula. op. cit., p. 12; Moser, Caroline O.N. & Clark, Fiona C. op. cit., p. 9; Puechguirbal, Nadine. *'Peacekeeping, Peacebuilding and Post-conflict Reconstruction'*.

Since the 1980s and 1990s, actors such as the United Nations and unilateral donors increasingly promoted gender sensitivity and gender mainstreaming in fields related to peace, conflict and security in the international system. Among other things, several resolutions concerning women and issues of peace and security were voted by the Security Council, which culminated into the resolution 1325 in 2000. Besides, other measures, such as the Convention on the Elimination of All Forms of Discrimination against Women (CEDAW), the African Women Committee on Peace and Development or the World Conferences on Women came into being.[30]

In conclusion of this section, some critical remarks regarding gender in peacemaking and peacebuilding are necessary. Notions of gender sensitivity tend to be based on Euro-American political and cultural values, which are of recent origin and normatively charged.[31] Non-Western feminists criticise white academics that assign their Western concepts of gender to other parts of the world, e.g. Africa, without asking if their occidental assumptions are valid elsewhere for being imperialist and 'First World-ist'.[32] Effectively, differentiation and contextualisation regarding gender are necessary because concepts

---

In: Shepherd, Laura J. (ed.). *Gender Matters in Global Politics. A Feminist Introduction to International Relations*. Abingdon, Routledge, 2010, pp. 163-165, 168. See also Gesellschaft für technische Zusammenarbeit (GTZ). *Towards Gender Mainstreaming in Crisis Prevention and Conflict Management: Guidelines for the German Technical Cooperation*. Eschborn, 2001; UNSC. op. cit., *Resolution*; United Nations Women. *Beijing and its Follow-up* [Website]. 2011. Available online at: http://www.un.org/womenwatch/daw/followup/beijing+5.htm (Accessed on 22 April 2011).

[30] Anderlini, Sanam Naraghi. *Women at the Peace Table: Making a Difference*. New York, United Nations Development Fund for Women, 2000, pp. 5-9, 45-50; Bouta, Tsjeard et al. op. cit., pp. 50-51; Hunt, Swanee & Posa, Christina. 'Women Waging Peace: Inclusive Security'. In: *Foreign Policy*, May/June, 2001, p. 38; United Nations General Assembly. *Convention on the Elimination of All Forms of Discrimination against Women* [Website]. 2011. Available online at: http://www.un.org/womenwatch/daw/cedaw/text/econvention.htm (Accessed on 27 June 2011); UNSC. op. cit., *Resolution 1325*.

[31] Agathangelou, Anna M. & Turcotte, Heather M. 'Postcolonial Theories and Challenges to ,First World-ism''. In: Shepherd, Laura J. (ed.). *Gender Matters in Global Politics. A Feminist Introduction to International Relations*. Abingdon, Routledge, 2010, pp. 47, 49-52; Pattynama, Pamela. 'Strangers and Double Self-consciousness: Feminism and Black Studies'. In: Buikema, Rosemarie & Smelik, Anneke. *Women's Studies and Culture: A Feminist Introduction*. London, Zed Books, 1993, pp. 138-139, 143.

[32] See Agathangelou, Anna M. & Turcotte, Heather M., op. cit.

of gender vary regionally and culturally.[33] Not only can Western interpretations of gender questions contravene traditional and customary practices and structures that continue to have a major impact in non-Western societies, but these societies might also face more urgent structural challenges than the ones related to gender.[34] This renders the already challenging acceptance and implementation of the latter even more difficult. In addition, progress that is made in terms of gender sensitivity must be measured against the respective background. Developments that seem relatively small compared to Western standards can represent great changes elsewhere and should be perceived accordingly.[35]

2.2. The impact of masculinity/masculinities as an obstacle to gender-sensitive post-conflict orders

Theoretical and normative assumptions that women's participation in peacemaking and peacebuilding leads to a gender-sensitive outcome or even a "feminist transformation"[36] do not seem to apply to Liberia. Hence, one has to identify theoretical approaches to explain this. Doubtlessly, changes regarding gender concern both women and men. Therefore, it is important to (re-) focus on the relation between the genders and to include men in analyses. This is why, the concept of masculinity/masculinities will be introduced here, whose influence plays in various ways an important role within (post-)conflict

---

[33] Agathangelou, Anna M. & Turcotte, Heather M., op. cit., pp. 47, 49-52; Morrel, Robert & Ouzgane, Lahoucine. 'African Masculinities: An Introduction'. In: Ouzgane, Lahoucine & Morrel, Robert (eds.). *African Masculinities: Men in Africa from the Late Nineteenth Century to the Present*. Basingstoke, Palgrave Macmillan, 2005, pp. 9, 18; Pattynama, Pamela. op. cit., pp. 138-139, 143. "'[W]omanhood' and 'manhood' [vary] with multiple scales such as constructions and geographies of power along racial, ethnic, class, sexual, regional and international dimensions". Agathangelou, Anna M. & Turcotte, Heather M., op. cit., p. 50.

[34] Agathangelou, Anna M. & Turcotte, Heather M. op. cit., p. 50.

[35] Richards, Paul. 'Young Men and Gender in War and Postwar Reconstruction: Some Comparative Findings from Liberia and Sierra Leone. In: Bannon, Ian & Correia, Maria C. (eds.). *The Other Half of Gender: Men's Issues in Development*. Washington D.C., The World Bank, 2006, p. 195.

[36] Bell, Christine & O'Rourke, Catherine as quoted in Hamber, Brandon. 'Masculinity and Transitional Justice: An Exploratory Essay'. In: *The International Journal of Transitional Justice*, Vol. 1, 2007, p. 37.

contexts.[37] It helps to better understand outcomes of certain policies after conflicts and, more precisely, to identify reasons that explain why the Liberian post-conflict social order has not become more gender-sensitive than it effectively is.[38] In the following paragraph, the notions of masculinity/masculinities and patriarchy will be defined and explained first. Then the structural significance of masculinities for institutions will be assessed and, finally, the relation between masculinities and violence will be explored.

Masculinity refers to "[c]haracteristics and modes of behaviour associated with being male"[39] and manhood. More precisely, masculinity consists of

> "behaviours, languages and practices, existing in specific cultural and organisational locations, which are commonly associated with males and thus culturally defined as not feminine."[40]

Consequently, masculinity does not exist naturally or biologically,[41] but it is created and produced within a social environment and through social practices, processes – including war – as well as factors such as agency, norms or expectations towards men.[42] Masculinity should not be seen as isolated from, but rather as interacting with femininity. Masculinity is constructed by and within the gender system, which means that women as well as notions of

---

[37] The encompassing discussion of masculinity and its creation is beyond the scope of this work. Here, solely the effects and impacts of masculinity in the context of conflict and its aftermath are discussed.

[38] Hamber, Brandon. op. cit., p. 377; Zalewski, Marysia & Parpart, Jane L. 'Introduction: Rethinking the Man Question'. In: Parpart, Jane L. & Zalewski, Marysia (eds.). *Rethinking the Man Question: Sex, Gender and Violence in International Relations*. London, Zed Books, 2008, p. 2.

[39] Shepherd, Laura J. 'Glossary'. In: ibid. (ed.). *Gender Matters in Global Politics. A Feminist Introduction to International Relations*. Abingdon, Routledge, 2010, pp. xxii.

[40] Whitehead, Stephen M. & Barrett, Frank J. as quoted in Hamber, Brandon. op. cit., p. 379. See also Hearn, Jeff. 'Masculinity/Masculinities'. In: Flood, Michael et al. *International Encyclopedia of Men and Masculinities*. London, Routledge, 2007, pp. 390-391.

[41] That is to say that it is not necessary to be male in order to be masculine.

[42] Connell, Raewyn W. *The Men and the Boys*. Cambridge, Polity Press, 2000, p. 216; Connell, Raewyn W. op. cit., *Masculinities*, pp. 71, 81; Enloe, Cynthia. op. cit., p. 3; Hamber, Brandon. op. cit., p. 379; Morrel, Robert & Ouzgane, Lahoucine. op. cit., pp. 4-9; Pankhurst, Donna. op. cit., 'Post-War Backlash Violence against Women', p. 295; Pankhurst, Donna. 'Sexual Violence in War'. In: Shepherd, Laura J. (ed.). *Gender Matters in Global Politics. A Feminist Introduction to International Relations*. Abingdon, Routledge, 2010, pp. 154, 157. For a more detailed analysis of different approaches to the conceptualisation of masculinity, see Connell, Raewyn W. op. cit., *Masculinities*, pp. 68-71.

femininity are involved in its formation.[43] It is more appropriate to use the plural form and speak of masculinities because there is not a single masculinity. When the term is employed in singular in the following, it is exclusively done for language reasons and does not consider masculinity as monolithic.

Masculinities like concepts of gender vary over time and in different societies and cultures. They are not internally homogeneous, but can differ between age groups, classes or ethnicities.[44] These various masculinities are structured by hierarchical power relations. There is often a *hegemonic masculinity*, which is "the most honoured or desired"[45] masculinity "that occupies the hegemonic position in a given pattern of gender relations."[46] For it is not necessarily the most expanded type that dominates more subordinated and marginalised forms of masculinity, certain masculinities – and thus men – are subordinated.[47]

Here, the notion of patriarchy needs to be introduced, too, because it is caused by specific masculine characteristics and because "patriarchal gender relations [are] both cause and consequence of war".[48] Patriarchy is the structural, although not monolithic, domination of men over women in various spheres. It results from "power and authority of masculinity"[49] and deliberate interaction of men and women. Losses and gains (the so-called *patriarchal*

---

[43] Cohn, Carol & Enloe, Cynthia. 'A Conversation with Cynthia Enloe: Feminists Look at Masculinity and the Men Who Wage War'. In: *Signs*, Vol. 28, No. 4, 2003, pp. 1188, 1199; Goldstein, Joshua S. op. cit., pp. 306-316; Hamber, Brandon. op. cit., p. 379; Pillay, Anu. op. cit., 'Violence against Women in the Aftermath', p. 41.

[44] Alsop, Rachel; Fitzsimons, Annette & Lennon, Kathleen. *Theorizing Gender*. Cambridge, Polity Press, 2002, p. 136-140; Barker, Gary, Ricardo, Christine. *Young Men and the Construction of Masculinity in Sub-Saharan Africa: Implications for HIV/AIDS, Conflict, and Violence*. Washington D.C., The World Bank (Social Development Papers: Conflict Prevention and Reconstruction, No. 26), 2005. Available online at: http://www.hsrc.ac.za/Document-86.phtml (Accessed on 18 August 2011); Connell, Raewyn. op. cit., *The Men and the Boys*, pp. 8, 10; Connell, Raewyn W. op. cit., *Masculinities*, pp. 75-76; Hamber, Brandon. op. cit., p. 378; Pankhurst, Donna. op. cit., 'Post-War Backlash Violence against Women', pp. 295, 301-302.

[45] Connell, Raewyn W. op. cit., *The Men and the Boys*, p. 10.

[46] Connell, Raewyn W. op. cit., *Masculinities*, p. 76.

[47] Connell, Raewyn W. op. cit., *The Men and the Boys*, pp. 10, 216-217; Connell, Raewyn W. op. cit., *Masculinities*, p. 76; Hamber, Brandon. op. cit., p. 379.

[48] Cockburn, Cynthia. 'Militarism and War'. In: Shepherd, Laura J. (ed.). *Gender Matters in Global Politics: A Feminist Introduction to International Relations*. Abingdon, Routledge, 2010, p. 106. See also ibid., p. 108.

[49] Shepherd, Laura J. op. cit., 'Glossary', p. xxiii.

dividend) are unequally distributed between social groups, so that its benefiters have an interest in maintaining the unequal structures. One has to note that such an order does not only disadvantage women, but younger men are discriminated against by elder men. Masculinity is by no means necessarily connected with patriarchy and the power relations within patriarchies are too complex to be fully explored here. Hence, the concept has limitations on the individual level. Nevertheless, it helps to explain gender and power relations on the macro level and is especially useful in the context of this study, as it is often a feature of African societies.[50]

Masculinities are not only important at the individual and societal level. There are collective masculinities that play an important role for states, armies and even the international system, which are masculine or masculinised.[51] This is due, in theoretical terms, to the absence of women in political theory related to them and, in practice, to the gender regime and the division of labour between men and women within these structures.[52] However, the relation between these collective bodies and masculinity is complex and reciprocal as "different kinds of masculinity are constructed within institutions and [...] masculinity is mobilized to meet the institutions' ends."[53] An example for this is the security sector that is often strongly shaped by a certain (hegemonic and potentially militarised) masculinity. At the same time, specific features of manhood are promoted within it for strategic purposes and are difficult to over-

---

[50] Connell, Raewyn W. op. cit., *Masculinities*, p. 82; Pankhurst, Donna. op. cit., 'Post-War Backlash Violence against Women', pp. 299-300; Pillay, Anu. op. cit., 'Violence against Women in the Aftermath' p. 39; Rahman, Najat. 'Patriarchy'. In: Flood, Michael et al. (eds.). *International Encyclopedia of Men and Masculinities*. London, Routledge, 2007, pp. 468-469; Whitehead, Stephen M. 'Patriarchal Dividend'. In: Flood, Michael et al. *International Encyclopedia of Men and Masculinities*. London, Routledge, 2007, p. 468.

[51] Bouta, Tsjeard et al. op. cit., p. 51; Cohn, Carol & Enloe, Cynthia. op. cit., p. 1188; Connell, Raewyn W. op. cit., *The Men and the Boys*, pp. 11, 213, 215-217; 220-223; Connell, Raewyn W. op. cit., *Masculinities*, pp. xx-xxi, 72-73; Enloe, Cynthia. op. cit., pp. 10, 195-196; Hearn, Jeff. 'Violence, Organisational and Collective'. In: Flood, Michael et al. *International Encyclopedia of Men and Masculinities*. London, Routledge, 2007, p. 619; Higate, Paul. 'Military Institutions'. In: Flood, Michael et al. *International Encyclopedia of Men and Masculinities*. London, Routledge, 2007, p. 441; Rahman, Najat. op. cit., p. 470; Zalewski, Marysia. op. cit., p. 35.

[52] Connell, Raewyn W. *Gender*. Cambridge, Polity Press, 2002, pp. 102-104.

[53] Cohn, Carol & Enloe, Cynthia. op. cit., pp. 1198-1199. See also Connell, Raewyn W. op. cit., *The Men and the Boys*, p. 216.

come.[54] Thus, institutions continue to exclude women or incorporate them only in a marginalised, patriarchal way. With regard to peace processes, which are dominated by these very masculine bodies, this potentially means that women as well as their needs are absent or underrepresented.

There are also relationships between masculinity and violence.[55] Here, one has to note that – although violence is predominantly committed by men – not all men or forms of masculinities are aggressive or violent. It was argued above that masculinities are not static; instead, they are modified by social, economic and political factors. The way how these factors change during or after a conflict affects masculinities. Furthermore, "violent patterns of masculinity develop in response to violence".[56] This means that the experience of armed conflicts can in certain cases provoke more aggressive behavioural patterns. Often, violent masculinities are even deliberately promoted by institutions, e.g. armed groups or states. Such developments impact on the nature of masculine post-conflict behaviour because there is continuity between masculinities in war-time and peace-time.[57] Collective violence within organisational cultures and structures and even individual violence is likely to persist after a conflict has ended and although practices, which were socially acceptable during a conflict, are deprecated in its aftermath. Besides, individuals or institutions can actively resist returning to more peaceful behaviour if this contradicts their interests.[58]

---

[54] Cohn, Carol & Enloe, Cynthia. op. cit., p. 1204; Connell, Raewyn W. op. cit., *The Men and the Boys*, p. 213; Enloe, Cynthia. op. cit., p. 18; Hearn, Jeff. op. cit., 'Violence, Organisational and Collective', p. 619.

[55] See Pankhurst, Donna. op. cit., 'Post-War Backlash Violence against Women', pp. 295-304; Pringle, Keith. 'Violence'. In: Flood, Michael et al. (eds.) *International Encyclopedia of Men and Masculinities*. London, Routledge, 2007, pp. 612-615.

[56] Connell, Raewyn W. op. cit., *The Men and the Boys*, p. 224; Goldstein, Joshua S. op cit., pp. 290-291, 293.

[57] Connell, Raewyn W. op. cit., *The Men and the Boys*. pp. 217-218, 224-225; Hamber, Brandon. op. cit., p. 380; Hearn, Jeff. op. cit., 'Violence, Organisational and Collective', pp. 618-621; Pankhurst, Donna. op. cit., 'Post-War Backlash Violence against Women', pp. 305-306, 308-309.

[58] Connell, Raewyn W. op. cit., *The Men and the Boys*, pp. 13-14, 219; Enloe, Cynthia. op. cit., p. 3; Hamber, Brandon. op. cit., pp. 382-38; Hearn, Jeff. op. cit., 'Violence, Organisational and Collective', p. 621; Pillay, Anu. op. cit., 'Violence against Women in the Aftermath', p. 40; Zalewski, Marysia. op. cit., p. 39.

Not only modifications in masculinities themselves, but also changes in gender relations and power dynamics can cause violence, if they challenge the position as well as the interests of men.[59] During armed conflicts, women often assume new, formerly male roles and develop particular survival strategies. Consequently, they are better prepared for challenges in the transitional period. If men suffer from poverty or other forms of powerlessness after the conflict, for example, due to a weak economy or disarmament and demobilisation, they risk developing a feeling of frustration and incapability to meet expectations of masculinity. They then react violently – especially in the private sphere – in order to compensate the suffered or perceived loss of manhood, correct gender relations and reassert domination.[60] Such a tendency can equally be provoked by – actual or seeming – empowerment of women. This means that such policies can have adverse consequences for women that were initially not intended. Furthermore, measures taken on the state and public level might provoke reactions at the individual and private level. However, not only women's empowerment, but also their increased poverty after conflict can facilitate aggressive behaviour. Economically marginalised and dependent women are more likely to suffer from gendered violence, as they do not have the opportunity to leave abusive relationships or are obliged to exchange sexual services for goods or shelter.[61]

---

[59] Alsop, Rachel, Fitzsimons, Annette & Lennon, Kathleen. op. cit., pp.134-135; Connell, Raewyn W. op. cit., *Masculinities*, pp. 82-84; Connell, Raewyn W. op. cit., *The Men and the Boys*, pp. 20-21, 217; Pankhurst, Donna. op. cit., 'Post-War Backlash Violence against Women', pp. 303, 307; Whitehead, Stephen M. op. cit., pp. 467-468.

[60] Connell, Raewyn W. op. cit., *Masculinities*, pp. 86-89; Hamber, Brandon. op. cit., pp. 384-385; Pankhurst, Donna. op. cit., 'Post-War Backlash Violence against Women', pp. 300, 311; Pillay, Anu. op. cit., 'Violence against Women in the Aftermath', pp. 40-41; Seidler, Victor. 'Masculinity and Violence'. In: May, Larry et al. (eds.). *Rethinking Masculinity: Philosophical Explorations in Light of Feminism*. London, Rowman & Littlefield, 1996, pp. 66-67, 69.

[61] Amnesty International (AI). *Rwanda: "Marked for Death", Rape Survivors Living with HIV/AIDS in Rwanda*. 2004, p. 9. Available online at: http://www.amnesty.org/en/library/asset/AFR47/007/2004/en/53d74ceb-d5f7-11dd-bb24-1fb85fe8fa05/afr4700720 04en.pdf (Accessed on 23 June 2011); Cockburn, Cynthia. op. cit., 'The Gendered Dynamics of Armed Conflict and Political Violence', p. 26; Hamber, Brandon. op. cit., pp. 382-383; Pankhurst, Donna. op. cit., 'Introduction', p. 6; Pankhurst, Donna. op. cit., 'Post-War Backlash Violence against Women', p. 300; Pillay, Anu. op. cit., 'Violence against Women in the Aftermath', p. 42.

In sum, there are various connections between masculinity patterns and male violence against women; however, they are often insufficiently analysed and need further consideration.[62] Certain features of masculinities, e.g. aggressiveness or militarisation, and their relations with femininities can help to understand the emergence of violence, especially in the light of increased participation of women and are thus of explanatory relevance here.[63]

Nevertheless, the integration of masculinities into the analysis of (post-) conflict contexts is not unproblematic and should not be oversimplified. Although violence is predominantly committed by men, not all men or forms of masculinities are aggressive or violent, as Connell underlines: "In any cultural setting, violent and aggressive masculinity will rarely be the only form of masculinity present".[64] Firstly, this means that masculinity does not naturally cause aggressive or violent behaviour. Essentialism should therefore be avoided. Secondly, influences of masculinity are never the only reasons for increased levels of violence or backlashes in gender relations after conflicts.[65] Moreover, some scholars argue that masculinity will distract the attention from women and women's issues and is thus understood as a setback increasing the probability of a backlash to the detriment of women.[66] This can be countered by the argument that men and masculinities can be at the origin of problems such as gendered violence and gender inequality.[67] If this is the case, approaches to solving the problems should include men and masculini-

---

[62] Hearn, Jeff. op. cit., 'Violence, Organisational and Collective', p. 621.
[63] A detailed analysis of the multi-causal and multidimensional relations of masculinity and violence as well as of the various types of male violence is beyond the scope of this chapter. For more information, see Pringle, Keith. op. cit., pp. 612-615.
[64] Connell, Raewyn W. op. cit., The Men and the Boys, p. 216.
[65] At the same time, the essentialist argument based on biological assumptions that all women are peaceful must be rejected. It is rather important to focus on social factors underlying the construction of masculinities and femininities. Ibid., pp. 215-216, 223-224; Connell, Raewyn W. op. cit., Masculinities, p. xv; Hearn, Jeff. op. cit., 'Violence, Organisational and Collective', p. 620; Pankhurst, Donna. op. cit. 'Post-War Backlash Violence against Women', pp. 296-297; Pringle, Keith. op. cit., p. 613. Factors that are likely to provoke a backlash for women after conflicts are presented by Pankhurst, Donna. op. cit., 'Post-War Backlash Violence against Women', pp. 294-295.
[66] Hamber, Brandon. op. cit., p. 387.
[67] Alsop, Rachel; Fitzsimons, Annette & Lennon, Kathleen. op. cit., pp.134-135; Connell, Raewyn W. op. cit., Masculinities, pp. 82-84; Connell, Raewyn W. op. cit., The Men and the Boys, pp. 20-21, 217; Pankhurst, Donna. op. cit., 'Post-War Backlash Violence against Women', pp. 303, 307; Whitehead, Stephen M. op. cit., pp. 467-468.

ties.[68] "[P]ractices and policies which fuel and flow from violent masculinities"[69] must be addressed, understood and criticised in order to be overcome. Additionally, there is a "security-insecurity cycle",[70] meaning that improved women's security in certain domains can provoke violence and thus increased insecurity in others. This underlines the necessity to include men and masculinities into policies to avoid negative outcomes at women's expense.[71]

2.3. Literature review

Following on from the theoretical background, this section reviews literature concerning gender-sensitive peacemaking and peacebuilding and their interconnection with masculinity studies. The objective is to identify theoretical shortcomings and weaknesses of the existing literature by portraying the development of the gender approach towards issues of peace and conflict.

For a long time, peace and conflict studies as well as international relations were largely gender-blind or even masculinised. Tickner states that

> "international politics is such a thoroughly masculinized sphere of activity that women's voices are considered inauthentic [...]. The values and assumptions that drive our contemporary international system are intrinsically related to concepts of masculinity; privileging these values constrains the options available to states and their policy-makers."[72]

Thus, women and gender issues were not only neglected concerning conflicts and international politics, but concepts, structures, actors or institutions were perceived and defined in a purely male-orientated way.[73]

In the 1970s, feminist scholars started to have greater theoretical influence, but the concept of gender was often included into existing literature in an essentialist way, so that the contribution was limited. Prevailing perceptions of

---

68 Hamber, Brandon. op. cit., pp. 383, 387.
69 Morrel, Robert as quoted in Hamber, Brandon. op. cit., p. 387.
70 Hamber, Brandon. op. cit., p. 385.
71 Connell, Raewyn W. op. cit., *Masculinities*, pp. 385-387.
72 Tickner, Ann as quoted in Jones, Adam. op. cit., p. 408.
73 Bouta, Tsjeard et al. op. cit., p. 51; Goldstein, Joshua S. op. cit., pp. 34-36, 53-57; Jones, Adam. op. cit., pp. 405, 408, 415. See also Parpart, Jane L. & Zalewski, Marysia (eds.). *Rethinking the Man Question: Sex, Gender and Violence in International Relations*. London, Zed Books, 2008; Steans, Jill. op. cit.

gender roles were reinforced by the supposed dualism of men waging wars and peaceful, comparatively passive women being victims.[74] Such a perspective does not reflect the complexity of conflicts, as women participate in various ways – not only as peacemakers, but also as fighters or supporters of warring factions – which is why a comprehensive and constructionist approach is imperative.[75] Works of Cynthia Enloe among others, finally helped to establish a feminist perspective on international politics and conflict research.[76]

Nowadays, the relevance of gender for war and peace is intensively dealt with by a wide range of both academic and policy-orientated literature, including publications by the United Nations (UN), other international organisations and national development agencies, such as the Department for International Development (DFID) or the German Technical Cooperation (GTZ).[77] In a broad sense, the literature can be categorised in publications focusing on women in wartime, in peace processes and in the post-conflict period. For the purpose of the present analysis, especially works on gender in the making and building of peace is relevant.[78] The theoretical and normative perspective is complimented by empirical works on women's roles in conflicts and their af-

---

[74] Badmus, Alani. op. cit., pp. 810-811; Giles, Wenona & Hyndman, Jennifer. op. cit., p. 4; Goldstein, Joshua S. op. cit., pp. 36-49.

[75] Alison, Miranda H. *Women and Political Violence. Female Combatants in Ethnonational Conflicts*. Abingdon, Routledge, 2009, pp. 85-88; Badmus, Alani. op. cit., pp. 811-812; Harders, Cilja. op. cit., pp. 240, 242-243; Mordt, Gabriele. op. cit., p. 63; Zalewski, Marysia. op. cit., p. 31.

[76] Elshtain, Jean Bethke. *Women and War*. Brighton, The Harvester Press, 1987; Enloe, Cynthia. op. cit. See also Pankhurst, Donna. op. cit., 'Introduction', pp. 1-30.

[77] Anderlini, Sanam Naraghi. op. cit., pp. 45-50; Bouta, Tsjeard et al. op. cit., pp. 50-51; Derbyshire, Helen. *Gender Manual: A Practical Guide for Development Policy Makers and Practitioners*. London, Department for International Development, 2002, Available online at: http://www.allindiary.org/pool/resources/dfid-gender-manual.pdf (Accessed on 11 May 2011); GTZ. op. cit., *Towards Gender Mainstreaming in Crisis Prevention*; Hunt, Swanee & Posa, Christina. op. cit., 2001, p. 38; United Nations General Assembly. op. cit., *Convention on the Elimination of All Forms of Discrimination against Women*; UNSC. op. cit., *Resolution 1325*; United Nations Women. op. cit., *Beijing and its Follow-up*.

[78] Baksh, Rawwida. 'Gender Mainstreaming in Post-conflict Reconstruction'. In Baksh, Rawwida et al. (eds.). *Gender Mainstreaming in Conflict Transformation: Building Sustainable Peace*. London, Commonwealth Secretariat, 2005, pp. 82-98; Ramsbotham, Oliver; Woodhouse, Tom & Miall, Hugh. op. cit., pp. 265-274.

termath, many of which concentrate their attention on specific regions.[79] However, some scholars note that despite the increasing variety of studies, there remains a lack of structured analysis of women's real contribution to the creation of peace.[80]

Researchers such as Donna Pankhurst, Carolyn Nordstrom and Anu Pillay focus on another fundamental aspect – the problem of increased domestic and sexual violence against women after armed conflicts or the 'backlash' of gender roles (where they had evolved into female empowerment during conflicts).[81] In this context, seemingly peaceful situations are criticised and gender-sensitive perspectives added to conventional concepts.[82] Their works indicate that the situation of women often deteriorates after conflicts and that the realisation of a gender-sensitive post-conflict order is much more difficult than often assumed.[83] They look for reasons that explain these tendencies.

---

[79] See, for example African Women and Peace Support Group. *Liberian Women Peacemakers: Fighting for the Right to Be Seen, Heard, and Counted*. Trenton, Africa World Press, 2004; Badmus, Alani. op. cit., pp. 808-839; George, Kla Emmanuel Gamoe. *Women as Agents of Peace during the Civil Wars in Liberia and Sierra Leone, 1989-2005*. Undated. (Mimeographed Paper). Available online at: www.isud.typepad.com/ files/george1.doc (Accessed on 28 April 2011); Nordstrom, Carolyn. op. cit., pp. 14-33; Pedersen, Jennifer. 'In the Rain and in the Sun: Women in Peacebuilding in Liberia'. *International Studies Association Annual Convention on Bridging Multiple Divides*. San Francisco, 26-29 March 2008. Available online at: http://www.allacademic.com//meta/ p_mla_apa_research_citation/2/5/3/1/3/pages253135/p253135-1.php (Accessed on 25 April 2011); Solomon, Christiana. 'The Mano River Union Sub-region: The Role of Women in Building Peace'. In: Baksh, Rawwida et al. (eds.). *Gender Mainstreaming in Conflict Transformation: Building Sustainable Peace*. London, Commonwealth Secretariat, 2005, pp. 171-180; Svensson, Katja. 'Women Hold up Half the Sky: Peace and Security. Lessons from Liberia'. In: *African Security Review*, Vol. 17, No. 4, 2008, pp. 178-183; Turshen, Meredeth & Twagiramariya, Clotilde (eds.). *What Women Do in Wartime: Gender and Conflict in Africa*. London, Zed Books, 1998.

[80] Solomon, Christiana. op. cit., p. 171; See also GTZ. op. cit., *Towards Gender Mainstreaming in Crisis Prevention*, p. 6.

[81] Nordstrom, Carolyn. op. cit.; Pankhurst, Donna. op. cit., 'Introduction', pp. 1-30; Pankhurst, Donna. op. cit.. 'Post-War Backlash Violence against Women', pp. 293-320; Pankhurst, Donna. op. cit., 'Sexual Violence in War', pp. 148-159; Pillay, Anu. op. cit., 'Violence against Women in the Aftermath', pp. 35-45.

[82] See Cockburn, Cynthia. op. cit., 'The Gendered Dynamics of Armed Conflict and Political Violence', pp. 13-29; Cockburn, Cynthia. op. cit., 'The Continuum of Violence', pp. 24-44; Nordstrom, Carolyn. op. cit., pp. 14-33.

[83] Bop, Codou. 'Women in Conflicts: Their Gains and Their Losses'. In: Meintjes, Sheila; Pillay, Anu & Turshen, Meredeth (eds.). *The Aftermath: Women in Post-Conflict Transformation*. London, Zed Books, 2001, pp. 20-25, 27-33; Meintjes, Sheila. 'War and Post-War Shifts in Gender Relations'. In: Meintjes, Sheila; Pillay, Anu & Turshen,

Among these are the problematic economic situation of men and women, underlying power relations, and social structures or traditions. Impacts of masculinities in and after conflicts are also attracting more and more academic attention.[84] But it must be noted that masculinity theory is still a developing field particularly in the African context.[85]

A lot was written on both the roles of women in peace processes and on their critical situation in the aftermath.[86] Nevertheless, it is difficult to identify analyses that combine these two positions and trace empirically, whether or not women's contributions to peace processes lead indeed to a more gender-sensitive peace compared to conventional approaches of conflict transfor-

---

Meredeth (eds.). *The Aftermath: Women in Post-Conflict Transformation*. London, Zed Books, 2001, pp. 63-77; Pankhurst, Donna. op. cit., 'Sexual Violence in War', pp. 149-150; Pankhurst, Donna. op. cit., 'Introduction', pp. 1-30; Pillay, Anu. op. cit., 'Violence against Women in the Aftermath', pp. 35-45.

[84] See, for example Hamber, Brandon. op. cit.; Large, Judith. op. c Large, Judith. 'Disintegration Conflicts and the Restructuring of Masculinity'. In: *Gender and Development*, Vol. 5, No. 2, 1997, pp. 23-30; Pankhurst, Donna. op. cit., 'Sexual Violence in War'; Pillay, Anu. op. cit., 'Violence against Women in the Aftermath', pp. 35-45.

[85] Hamber, Brandon. op. cit., p. 377.

[86] For example, refer to African Women and Peace Support Group. *Liberian Women Peacemakers: Fighting for the Right to Be Seen, Heard, and Counted*. Trenton, Africa World Press, 2004; Anderlini, Sanam Naraghi. op. cit.; Baksh, Rawwida et al. (eds.). op. cit; Bekoe, Dorina & Parajon, Christina. *Women's Role in Liberia's Reconstruction* [Website]. Washington D.C., United States Institute for Peace, 2007. Available online at: http://www.usip.org/publications/women-s-role-liberia-s-reconstruction (Accessed on 20 August 2011); Bouta, Tsjeard et al. op. cit.; Cockburn, Cynthia. op, cit., 'The Gendered Dynamics of Armed Conflict and Political Violence'; Cockburn, Cynthia. op. cit., 'The Continuum of Violence; Fleshman, Michael. 'African Women Struggle for a Seat at the Peace Table'. In: *Africa Renewal* [Website], Vol. 16, No. 4, 2003. Available online at: http://www.un.org/ecosocdev/geninfo/afrec/vol16no4/164wm1.htm (Accessed on 25 April 2011); George, Kla Emmanuel Gamoe. op. cit.; Hunt, Swanee & Posa, Christina. op. cit.; Jones, Katelyn. op. cit.; Meintjes, Sheila; Pillay, Anu & Turshen, Meredeth (eds.). *The Aftermath: Women in Post-Conflict Transformation*. London, Zed Books, 2001; Pankhurst, Donna (ed.). *Gendered Peace: Women's Struggles for Post-War Justice and Reconciliation*. London, Routledge, 2008; Pedersen, Jennifer. op. cit.; Puechguirbal, Nadine. op. cit.; Solomon, Christiana. op. cit.; Sweetman, Caroline (ed.). *Gender, Peacebuilding and Reconstruction*. Oxford, Oxfam GB, 2005; Turshen, Meredeth & Twagiramariya, Clotilde (eds.). *What Women Do in Wartime: Gender and Conflict in Africa*. London, Zed Books, 1998; Väyrynen, Tarja. op. cit., 'Women of Liberia's Mass Action for Peace'. In: *The Scavenger: Salvaging What's Left after the Masses Have Had Their Feed*. Undated. Available online at: http://www.thescavenger.net/people/women-of-liberias-mass-action-for-peace-37462-315.html (Accessed on 07 June 2012).

mation and examine the underlying causalities. The study at hand will concentrate on this gap in the literature and include an analytical and empirical perspective to the often normative discourse about women in peacemaking and peacebuilding that dominates the academic and political sphere.

In this chapter, theories of gender sensitivity, theories of peace from a feminist perspective, theories of peacemaking and peacebuilding and theories of masculinity and gender-based violence were outlined. Additionally, the state of the research was explored. This sets the scene for the following empirical part of the analysis.

3. Liberia's past and present: An overview of Liberian history from the foundation to the early 2000s

This chapter begins with a general, socio-cultural account of Liberian history, goes on to outline Liberian gender order and ends by recounting the Liberian conflict of 1989-2003. A deeper knowledge of Liberian history will facilitate a better understanding of recent developments and tendencies relating to gendered peace in subsequent analysis chapters.

3.1. Review of the historical and socio-cultural background of Liberia

Liberia is a West African coastal country; with a total area of 97,754 square kilometres, it is roughly the same size as Hungary.[1] It shares boarders with Sierra Leone to the West, Guinea to the North and Côte d'Ivoire to the East (see Appendix I). It has a population of approximately 4.1 million people around a third of which live in the capital city, Monrovia.[2] Liberia was founded in 1822 by liberated African-Americans with the purpose of accommodating freed Black slaves from the United States and the Caribbean. These so-called Americo-Liberians made up approximately five per cent of the then 2.5 million inhabitants. The rest of the population were indigenous tribes divided into 16 ethnic groups,[3] most of which have connections to constituencies in neighbouring countries.[4]

---

[1] *Fischer Weltalmanach 2008.* Frankfurt am Main, Fischer Taschenbuch Verlag, 2007, p. 309.

[2] United Nations Development Programme (UNDP). *Liberia: Country Profile of Human Development Indicators* [Website]. New York, 2011. Available online at: http://hdrstats. undp.org/en/countries/profiles/LBR.html (Accessed on 18 June 2011).

[3] The biggest ethnic groups are the Kpelle (20 per cent), the Bassa (14 per cent) and the Grebo (9 per cent). The other 13 groups make up the remaining 57 per cent of the indigenous population, which highlights the ethnic diversification of the native Liberian population. *Fischer Weltalmanach 2008.* op. cit., p. 309.

[4] Adebajo, Adekeye. *Liberia's Civil War: Nigeria, ECOMOG, and Regional Security in West Africa.* London, Lynne Rienner Publishers, 2002, p. 21; *Fischer Weltalmanach 2008.* op. cit., p. 309; Bennett, Olivia et al. (eds.). *Arms to Fight, Arms to Protect: Women Speak out about Conflict.* London, Panos, 1995, p. 31; Richards, Paul. 'Young Men and Gender in War and Postwar Reconstruction: Some Comparative Findings

The country, although not being officially colonised, had strong connections to the United States of America from its beginnings.[5] With its declaration of independence in 1847, Liberia became the first African republic.[6] In effect, society was far from being characterised by republican or egalitarian values, as the Americo-Liberian settler minority established an oligarchic one-party system.[7] They ruled over the country in a corrupt and nepotistic way, oppressed and exploited the indigenous population that were kept politically and economically marginalised, although native Liberians obtained full citizenship in 1904.[8]

Under the presidencies of William S. Tubman and William R. Tolbert who governed the country from 1944 to 1971 and 1971 to 1980, respectively, some improvements were achieved. Under Tubman, a certain degree of development and unification of the country was effectuated, as he made efforts to overcome ethnic divisions and increased the participation and representation of indigenous Liberians.[9] Later, Tolbert continued reforms, for example in terms of education for the native population. Nevertheless, discrimination and inequality (four per cent of the population owned 60 per cent of the country's wealth) persisted. From the early 1970s, political opposition grew stronger and started to weaken Tolbert's rule. The situation deteriorated further, when Liberian proceeds from exports dropped because of falling commodity prices for the main export goods.[10] Liberia's foreign debt increased and it struggled to finance imports, especially food. In 1979, violent protests broke out be-

from Liberia and Sierra Leone. In: Bannon, Ian & Correia, Maria C. (eds.). *The Other Half of Gender: Men's Issues in Development*. Washington D.C., The World Bank, 2006, p. 197; UNDP. op. cit., *Liberia: Country Profile;* United States Agency for International Development (USAID). *Liberia: Country Profile*. Undated. Available online at: http://www.usaid.gov/locations/sub-saharan_africa/countries/liberia/liberia_profile.pdf (Accessed on 18 June 2011).
5   Fuest, Veronika. "This Is the Time to Get in Front': Changing Roles and Opportunities for Women in Liberia'. In: *African Affairs*, Vol. 107, No. 427, 2008, p. 204.
6   Adebajo, Adekeye. op. cit., *Liberia's Civil War*, p. 21; Fuest, Veronika. Op. cit., p. 205.
7   Adebajo, Adekeye. op. cit., *Liberia's Civil War*, p. 19.
8   ibid., pp. 21, 33; African Women and Peace Support Group. *Liberian Women Peacemakers: Fighting for the Right to Be Seen, Heard, and Counted*. Trenton, Africa World Press, 2004, pp. ix; Bennett, Olivia et al. (eds.). op. cit., pp. 26-27; Fuest, Veronika. op. cit., pp. 204-205; Richards, Paul. op. cit., pp. 198-199.
9   Adebajo, Adekeye. op. cit., *Liberia's Civil War*, pp. 21-22.
10 U.S. Department of State. *Background Note: Liberia* [Website]. 2011. Available online at: http://www.state.gov/r/pa/ei/bgn/6618.htm#history (Accessed on 27 August 2011).

cause of rising food prices, which sparked the beginning of the end of Tolbert's regime.[11]

In April 1980, Master-Sergeant Samuel K. Doe, a native Liberian, launched a coup d'état that led to the overthrow and assassination of Tolbert. This put an end to 133 years of Americo-Liberian political and economic domination marked by a difficulties emanating from "politics of ethnicity and clientelism, [an] anti-democratic political framework, socio-economic inequalities and underdevelopment".[12]

Doe's regime cannot be considered progress, because the political, societal and economic situation deteriorated. He established an autocratic and corrupt government that was responsible for the oppression and assassination of members of the opposition and human rights abuses. His power was based on an ethnic coalition of the Krahn, his own ethnicity, and the Mandingo. Together the two groups make up approximately twelve per cent of the indigenous population, which indicates the weak ethnic basis the regime was built on.[13] The Armed Forces of Liberia (AFL), formerly dominated by Americo-Liberians, were transformed into an ethnically partisan institution. As a consequence, ethnic divisions at all levels of society increased and Doe was highly unpopular among the majority of Liberians that continued to be marginalised by his new, ethnically based regime.[14] Although no longer in government, the Americo-Liberian elite remained in a better social situation compared to the indigenous population and kept exerting political influence. Fur-

---

[11] Adebajo, Adekeye. op. cit., *Liberia's Civil War*, pp. 19-23; Bennett, Olivia et al. (eds.). op. cit., pp. 26-27.

[12] Francis, David J. *The Politics of Economic Regionalism: Sierra Leone in ECOWAS*. Aldershot, Ashgate, 2001, p. 41. See also Adebajo, Adekeye. op. cit., *Liberia's Civil War*, pp. 19, 24-25; Howe, Herbert. 'Lessons from Liberia: ECOMOG and Regional Peacekeeping'. In: *International Security*, Vol. 21, No. 3, 1996, p. 147; Pitts, Michelle. 'Sub-Regional Solutions for African Conflict: The ECOMOG Experiment'. In: *The Journal of Conflict Studies* [Website], Vol. 19, No. 1, 1999. Available online at: http://journals.hil.unb.ca/index.php/JCS/article/view/4379/5057 (Accessed on 18 June 2011).

[13] Adebajo, Adekeye. op. cit., *Liberia's Civil War*, pp. 20, 42; Bennett, Olivia et al (eds.). op. cit., p. 26. *Fischer Weltalmanach 2008*. Frankfurt am Main, Fischer Taschenbuch Verlag, 2007.

[14] Adebajo, Adekeye. op. cit., *Liberia's Civil War*, pp. 20, 26-27, 29-30.

thermore, the economic situation did not improve and Liberia continued to suffer from economic decline and increasing debts.[15]

Weakened by these factors, Doe's regime began to crumble in the mid-1980s. 1985 was characterised by the organisation of elections that were rigged and led to the overwhelming, but implausible victory of Doe.[16] In the same year, there was a massacre by government troops in Nimba county claiming 3,000 Gio and Mano victims.[17] This intensified ethnic divides and re-sentments against the government that were later used by Charles Taylor, who benefited from support from Nimba county for his invasion.[18]
Another key factor promoting the war was the modification of the US-American position towards Liberia. At the end of the Cold War, the United States eventually withdrew their support for Doe's regime, because Liberia had lost its strategic importance in world politics. However, Samuel Doe de-pended heavily on the political, economic and military relationships with the superpower as well as its financial support. Its change in position did not only reinforce the precarious economic situation, but also created a security vacu-um facilitating Taylor's invasion of Liberia.[19]

The events of the nineteenth and twentieth century led to and consolidated an exclusive as well as discriminatory socio-political order and underlying ten-sions within the society that paved the way for the outbreak of the Liberian conflict in 1989. These factors became reinforced under the rule of Samuel

[15] ibid., p. 27; *Bird's-eye View of Liberian History and Government* [Website]. Undated. Available online at: http://www.africawithin.com/tour/liberia/hist_gov1.htm (Accessed on 28 August 2011).
[16] Adebajo, Adekeye. op. cit., *Liberia's Civil War*, pp. 28-29; Global Security. *Liberia – Election and Coup Attempt – 1985* [Website]. Undated. Available online at: http://www.globalsecurity.org/military/world/war/liberia-1985.htm (Accessed on 28 August 2011); Pitts, Michelle. op. cit.; U.S. Department of State. op. cit.
[17] Adebajo, Adekeye. op. cit., *Liberia's Civil War*, pp. 20, 28-29. The killings followed an attempted coup by a former General that was supported by the Gio (the General's eth-nicity) and the Mano. Global Security. op. cit.
[18] Adebajo, Adekeye. op. cit., *Liberia's Civil War*, p. 42.; Bennett, Olivia et al. (eds.). op. cit., p. 28.
[19] Adebajo, Adekeye. op. cit., *Liberia's Civil War*, pp. 33-36; Bennett, Olivia et al. (eds.). op. cit., p. 28.

Doe and finally culminated in a bloody civil strife that devastated the already problem-ridden and underdeveloped country for more than a decade.[20]

3.2. Women's socio-cultural position in pre-conflict Liberia

In addition to the general contemplation of Liberia's history, one has to study its gender regime in order to know what opportunities and room for manoeuvre women possess and in order to recognise to what extent their situation has changed after fourteen years of conflict. There are empirical findings that gender inequality and a high degree of gendered violence in a society is positively correlated with recourse to violence.[21] It is thus imperative to examine the societal dynamics in Liberia from a gendered perspective here.

Liberian society is traditionally patriarchal, patrimonial as well as patrilineal, and marked by strong gender inequality. Patriarchal refers to a social order, where the male head of the family possesses authority and power of decision over the entire family. Patrimonialism describes a form of governance based on personal rule instead of rational legal institutions and strengthened by political and economic patron-client relations, which are in the case of Liberia male-dominated. Patrilineal means that the lineage is determined by the father.[22] Although female roles developed in scope and independence as a consequence of macro-economic change, Liberian women's main responsibilities comprise farming, domestic work and child care. In many respects, they are traditionally subordinated to men, e.g. elders or husbands. According to customary law, a woman is perceived as her husband's property because

---

[20] Aboagye, Festus B. & Bah, Alhaji M. S. *Liberia at a Crossroads: A Preliminary Look at the United Nations Mission in Liberia (UNMIL) and the Protection of Civilians.* Pretoria, Institute of Security Studies (Occasional Paper No. 95), 2004. Available online at: http://www.iss.org.za/pubs/papers/95/Paper95.htm (Accessed on 28 June 2011).

[21] See Bouta, Tsjeard et al. *Gender, Conflict, and Development.* Washington D.C., The World Bank, 2005, p. 61; Caprioli, Mary. 'Gendered Conflict'. In: *Journal of Peace Research*, Vol. 37, No. 1, 2000, pp. 51-68; Caprioli, Mary & Boyer, Mark A. 'Gender, Violence, and International Crisis'. In: *The Journal of Conflict Resolution*, Vol. 45, No. 4, 2001, pp. 503-518.

[22] Fuest, Veronika. op. cit., p. 222; Meyers Lexikonredaktion (eds.) *Meyers Neues Lexikon: In zehn Bänden: 7. Band: N-Pra.* Mannheim, Meyers Lexikonverlag, 1993, p. 349; Richards, Paul. op. cit., pp. 202, 205; Schraeder, Peter J. *African Politics and Society: A Mosaic in Transformation.* Belmont, Wadsworth, 2004, p. 183.

of the high bride price he pays to her family before the marriage. This causes difficulties in various ways. On one side, girls are often married at a very young age to much older men and live in polygamous households. They are used to work in a slave-like way, provide reproductive services or to tie or consolidate patron-client-relationships.[23] On the other, they are obliged to stay in abusive relationships as their families cannot afford to pay back the bride price.[24] Besides, property rights were and remain "highly gender-asymmetric"[25] in customary law. Women are economically and socially de-pendant on male relatives. Consequently, divorced or widowed women do not have access to property, inheritance and custody of their children. After hav-ing examined the Liberian property and marriage system, Richards concluded that in many respects it was influenced by the previous slave system:

> "It can be argued that the extensive development of patron-client relations in postslavery Liberia [...] is less an expression of African social inclusiveness and family responsibility [...] than the survival of a system in which depend-ents are granted protection not through their rights as persons but through attachment to an owner."[26]

Hence, modern forms of slavery and dependence are created by persisting traditional practices such as sharecropping,[27] polygamy or dependent working as means to pay off debts, including dowry.[28] Not only does this create ine-quality between men and women, but also within one sex group between dif-ferent age cohorts. Young women and men both face social exclusion and are left entrapped as it is difficult to become economically independent or create a consensual family unit. This does not lead to social cohesion, but

---

[23] Richards, Paul. op. cit., pp. 201-203, 213.
[24] Amnesty International (AI). *Liberia: A Flawed Process Discriminates against Women and Girls.* 2008. Available online at: http://www.amnesty.org/en/library/asset/AFR34/00 4/2008/en/c075d220-00cf-11dd-a9d5-b31ac3ea5bcc/afr340042008eng.pdf (Accessed on 04 July 2011), p. 30; Bennett, Olivia et al. (eds.). op. cit., p. 42; Fuest, Veronika. op. cit., pp. 206-209; Richards, Paul. op. cit., pp. 201-204.
[25] Richards, Paul. op. cit., pp. 201-202.
[26] ibid., p. 202. See also ibid., p. 204.
[27] Sharecropping is a system, where a farmer pays for his or her rented land with part of his or her crop. See *Cambridge Dictionaries Online* [Website]. Cambridge, Cambridge University Press, 2011. Available online at: http://dictionary.cambridge.org/ (Accessed on 25 August 2011).
[28] Richards, Paul. op. cit., pp. 201-203, 213.

creates a suspense-packed social order, where youths are disadvantaged, that is aggravated by demographic incline.[29] Therefore, Fuest concludes that

> "the Liberian conflict seems to be rooted in multiple factors: traditionally hierarchical organizations based on the control of labour and marriage, which amounted to domestic slavery for many of those considered as junior dependants, in particular male and female youths [and] the hegemony of the Americo-Liberians."[30]

This underlines that a closer look at inter and intra-gender dynamics within Liberian society is essential to identifying tensions that contributed to the final outbreak of intra-state violence.

Girls are also disadvantaged regarding formal education. Before the war, only 30 per cent of pupils were female, in 2006 they made up 43 per cent.[31] In comparison to boys, girls were more likely to drop out prematurely, which means that very few reach and complete secondary education. They tended to be disproportionately affected by the shortage and poor quality of rural education, as they were less likely to be sent to schools in cities.[32] Altogether, the illiteracy rate of women (58 per cent) is more than twice as high as men's (27 per cent),[33] which adversely affects concerned women's and their de-

---

[29] ibid., pp. 203-205, 209. In Liberia, the median age is 18.3 years. 44.3 per cent of the Liberian population are aged 0-14. Central Intelligence Agency (CIA). *The World Factbook: Liberia* [Website]. 2011. Available online at: https://www.cia.gov/library/ publications/the-world-factbook/geos/li.html (Accessed on 26 August 2011).

[30] Fuest, Veronika. op. cit., p. 205. See also Richards, Paul. op. cit., p. 200.

[31] Fuest, Veronika. op. cit., p. 216-217. Although the percentage increased in absolute terms, this must be relativised as this is partly due to the demographic incline.

[32] George, Kla Emmanuel Gamoe. *Women as Agents of Peace During the Civil Wars in Liberia and Sierra Leone, 1989—2005.* Undated. (Mimeographed Paper). Available online at: www.isud.typepad.com/files/george1.doc (Accessed on 28 April 2011). United Nations General Assembly. *Liberia Is Writing New History for Its Women and Girls Delegation Tells Women's Anti-Discrimination Committee, Admitting Great Challenges in That Endeavour* [Website]. New York, 2009. Available online at: http://www.un.org/ News/Press/docs/2009/wom1748.doc.htm (Accessed on 20 July 2011). George calculates that 50 per cent of the girls drop out during primary and 30 per cent during secondary education. He further concludes that a maximum of five per cent accomplishes tertiary education and holds a first degree. George, Kla Emmanuel Gamoe. op. cit.

[33] CIA. op. cit. *The World Factbook.* Data regarding the female illiteracy rate in Liberia vary greatly. Some sources even estimate it at 81 per cent. Aisha, Fatoumata. 'Mainstreaming Gender in Peace Support Operations: The United Nations Mission in Liberia'. In: Aboagye, Festus & Bah, Alahji (eds.). *A Tortuous Road to Peace: The Dynamics of Regional, UN and International Humanitarian Interventions in Liberia.* Pretoria, Publications of the Institute of Security Studies, 2005, p. 147

pendants' lives, as they lack, among other things, entrepreneurial and employment skills and knowledge of healthcare provision.[34]

The role of women in Liberian society is, however, more differentiated and complex. It must be considered that they have attained a certain influence and scope of action thanks to female secret societies, the *Sande*. Their tasks include, for example, initiation, the preservation and passing on of knowledge and the preservation of the moral order. But here again, tensions between women of different generations occur, as youngsters subordinate to elders.[35] Furthermore, it is necessary to distinguish between Americo-Liberian and native women. Although the former did not benefit at all from equal rights to men, their (legal) situation was comparatively better than that of indigenous females. They – and very few native Liberia women – were better educated than the female (indigenous) majority, even attended universities, and started to gradually occupy professional and political positions to the detriment of Afro-Liberian men.[36] The social and educational status some Liberian women possess constitutes an important basis for the peace movement. A breakdown of women occupying prominent roles in women's organisations reveals that the majority were highly educated, usually studied in Europe or the USA and held leading social positions.[37]

In sum, the analysis of the Liberian gender order reveals women's discrimination. Tensions and hierarchies between and within the genders impacted on the outbreak of the conflict. The exceptional position of a minority of upcoming Americo-Liberian and very few native women shows that there is a tradition of Liberian females assuming responsibility and leadership, although not to be overestimated.[38] These findings contribute to understanding why the commitment of women in peacemaking was both remarkable and possible, and form a basis to evaluate gender sensitivity in the post-conflict order.

---

[34] African Women and Peace Support Group. op. cit., p. 6; Fuest, Veronika. op. cit., pp. 208-209, 216, 223; Richards, Paul. op. cit., pp. 212-213.
[35] African Women and Peace Support Group. op. cit., pp. 6-7; Fuest, Veronika. op. cit., pp. 206-207; Richards, Paul. op. cit., p. 200.
[36] Fuest, Veronika. op. cit., pp. 207-208. Richards, Paul. op. cit., p. 201.
[37] African Women and Peace Support Group. op. cit., pp. 95-98.
[38] Fuest, Veronika. op. cit., p. 223.

3.3. The outbreak and progression of the Liberian conflict (1989-2003)

The Liberian conflict consisted of two civil wars, which were strongly intertwined. The first one started in 1989 and reached settlement in 1997. However, the situation remained unstable. In 1999, violence increased again and led to another open war that lasted until 2003.

In December 1989, Charles Taylor and his rebel movement National Patriotic Front of Liberia (NPFL) invaded the country in order to overthrow the dictatorial regime of Samuel Doe, re-introduce democracy and national unity and to rebuild the Liberian economy.[39] The attack on Nimba county in the North East of Liberia was launched from Ivorian territory. Initially, the NPFL consisted of less than 200 fighters that comprised Gio, inhabitants from Nimba county and other nationals that had gone into exile in the sub-region, but in May 1990, it already ran up to 10,000 members.[40] In terms of arms, training and access to territory, the rebel movement was supported by Libya, Burkina Faso and Côte d'Ivoire.

---

[39] The information regarding to the first Liberian civil war is taken from the following sources, which are also to be consulted for a more detailed analysis of the events, as the latter is beyond the scope of this study: Aboagye, Festus B. & Bah, Alhaji M. S. op. cit.; Adebajo, Adekeye. *Building Peace in West Africa. Liberia, Sierra Leone, and Guinea-Bissau.* London, Lynne Rienner Publishers, 2002, pp. 43-78; Adebajo, Adekeye. op. cit., *Liberia's Civil War*, pp. 42-55, 57-59; Adebajo, Adekeye. 'West Africa's Tragic Twins. Building Peace in Liberia and Sierra Leone'. In: Keating, Tom & Knight, W. Andy (eds.). *Building Sustainable Peace.* Edmonton, University of Alberta Press, 2004, pp. 167-188; African Women and Peace Support Group. op. cit., pp. ix-xiii, 2-5; Al. op. cit., *Liberia: A Flawed Process*, p. 8; Aning, Emmanuel Kwesi. 'Peacekeeping under ECOMOG. A Sub-regional Approach'. In: Cilliers, Jakkie & Mills, Greg (eds.). *From Peacekeeping to Complex Emergencies: Peace Support Missions in Africa.* Johannesburg, South African Institute of International Affairs, 1999, pp. 85-95; Bennett, Olivia et al. (eds.). op. cit., p. 28; British Broadcasting Corporation (BBC). *Liberia Country Profile* [Website]. 2010. Available online at: http://news.bbc.co.uk/1/hi/world/africa/country _profiles/1043500.stm (Accessed on 18 June 2011); Cleaver, Gerry & Massey, Simon. 'Liberia: a Durable Peace at Last?' In: Furley, Oliver & May, Roy (eds.). *Ending Africa's Wars. Progressing to Peace.* Aldershot, Ashgate, 2006, pp. 179-199; Francis, David J. op. cit., pp. 40-44, 50-51; Howe, Herbert. op. cit., pp. 146-160; Pitts, Michelle. op. cit.

[40] For more information on the NPFL and Charles Taylor, see Adebajo, Adekeye. op. cit., *Liberia's Civil War*, pp. 58-59.

What followed was a complex and deadly civil strife, in which Doe's AFL, Taylor's NPFL, additional rebel movements[41] and from 1990 ECOMOG troops were involved sustaining their activities with the help of the extensive war economy that was based on natural resources (e.g. diamonds and precious wood species). The Liberian army reacted to the insurgence with brutality that did not only target the rebels but also civilians and led to the escalation of the conflict in 1990. As Taylor was mainly supported by Gio and Mano, whereas Doe's power was based on Krahn and Mandingo, the fighting was characterised by a strong inter-ethnic component. Over time, the splintering of rebel movements further complicated the conflict dynamics. In 1991, the National Patriotic Front of Liberia, the Independent National Patriotic Front of Liberia (INPFL) led by Yeduo Johnson and the United Movement for Democracy in Liberia (ULIMO) confronted each other, while two years later the number of conflict parties had more than doubled with the emergence of the Liberian United Democratic Front (LUDF), the Liberia Peace Council (LPC), the ULIMO-Kromah faction and the ULIMO-Johnson faction as well as the Lofa Defense Force (LDF).[42] Therefore, the situation grew more and more confusing, complicated and deadly. Furthermore, the fighting spread throughout Liberia including the capital Monrovia.

In August 1990, the ECOWAS launched a peacekeeping intervention because the humanitarian situation had deteriorated considerably. Refugee flows to other West African countries risked destabilising the entire sub-region.[43] Crucially, the international community did not take any action. However, at that time, there was no peace to keep anymore. Instead, the ECOWAS Monitoring Group (ECOMOG) had to take enforcement actions and became another contentious conflict party.[44] In September of the same year, Doe was killed by the INPFL. The violence, however, continued and even spilled over into Guinea and Sierra Leone.

---

[41] See below.
[42] See Pitts, Michelle. op. cit., Appendix I.
[43] Howe, Herbert. op. cit., p. 150.
[44] For a detailed analysis of the background and progression of the ECOMOG mission in Liberia, refer to Adebajo, Adekeye. op. cit., *Liberia's Civil War*, pp. 60-65; Aning, Emmanuel Kwesi. *Managing Regional Security in West Africa: Ecowas, Ecomog and Liberia.* Copenhagen, Centre for Development Research (Working Paper No. 94.2), 1994; Francis, David J. op. cit.; Howe, Herbert. op. cit., pp. 145-176; Pitts, Michelle. op. cit.

Between 1990 and 1997, nine ceasefires were negotiated and several transitional governments installed, but none was lasting.[45] Despite the eventual deployment of the United Nations Observer Mission in Liberia (UNOMIL) in 1993, the war continued until 1996, when the Abuja II Peace Agreement brought some stability and installed the third transitional government under Ruth Perry. In August 1997, Charles Taylor was elected President of Liberia defeating Ellen Johnson-Sirleaf.[46] The vote was generally considered to be free and fair, although it was dominated and decided by fear and the threat of more violence by the former warlord.[47] Once officially in power, Taylor formed the government and security forces from groups loyal to him. This harmed "national consensus and confidence in the country's faltering peace process".[48] Besides, major problems of the conflict-affected country and the structures that had developed during the war, such as the integration of rebel groups into the government, looting, the war economy as well as ethnic divisions, persisted. Combined with insufficient demobilisation and disarmament as well as political instability, these led to new violence in 1999. It escalated into the second civil war when the rebel movement Liberians United for Reconciliation and Democracy (LURD) took up weapons against Taylor and was later joined by the Movement for Democracy in Liberia (MODEL). The two factions controlled more and more of the Liberian territory and again caused serious humanitarian problems and refugee flows.[49]

Gradually, international pressure increased, including various UN resolutions and embargos against Liberia (e.g. UNSCR 1343, 1408 and 788) and the

---

[45] Aboagye, Festus B. & Bah, Alhaji M. S. op. cit.
[46] African Women and Peace Support Group. op. cit., p. xi.
[47] Pitts, Michelle. op. cit.
[48] Aboagye, Festus B. & Bah, Alhaji M. S. op. cit.
[49] For more details on the situation in Liberia after 1997 and the second civil war, see Aboagye, Festus B. & Bah, Alhaji M. S. op. cit.; Adebajo, Adekeye. op. cit., *Building Peace in West Africa*, pp. 67-73; African Women and Peace Support Group. op. cit., pp. ix-xiii; Al. op. cit., *Liberia*, pp. 8-9; Francis, David J. et al. *Dangers of Co-deployment: UN Co-operative Peacekeeping in Africa*. Aldershot, Ashgate, 2005, pp. 131-132. Gerdes, Felix. *Liberia* [Website]. Arbeitsgemeinschaft Kriegsursachenforschung, Hamburg. http://www.sozialwiss.uni-hamburg.de/publish/Ipw/Akuf/kriege/260 ak_liberia.htm (Accessed on 05 June 2011).

foundation of the International Contact Group on Liberia.[50] In June 2003, peace talks started in Accra and Akosombo, Ghana, leading to the Accra Ceasefire Agreement. Nevertheless, the fighting continued. On 21 July 2003, US troops arrived in Liberia. On 11 August, Taylor finally stepped down and fled into Nigerian exile. A week later, the Comprehensive Peace Agreement (CPA) was signed leading to the creation of a transitional government led by the civilian Gyude Bryant and clearing the way for another ECOWAS intervention (ECOMIL).[51] This was followed by the deployment of the United Nations Mission in Liberia (UNMIL) based on UNSCR 1497 and 1509.[52] In many regions of the country, violence continued until the end of 2003.

The signing of the peace accord was the beginning of the reconstruction and adaptation process for the country. But Liberians – especially women – continue being affected by the repercussions of the conflict. The gross domestic product per capita had dropped to only 222 US-Dollars per year, while external debts are overwhelming.[53] In the Human Development Index of 2010, Liberia ranks 162 out of 169 countries and has a Gender Inequality Index of

---

[50] The International Contact Group on Liberia was conceived as a forum putting pressure on the country. It consisted of Burkina Faso, Nigeria, Senegal, Ghana, Morocco, as well as Great Britain, France, the United States, the UN, EU, ECOWAS and the African Union.

[51] Major objectives of the CPA were the implementation of the ceasefire, the "deployment of [an] International Stabilisation Force" with a chapter VII mandate, a 2-year transitional government, the implementation of SSR and a DDRR programme. It also included issues on transitional justice and human rights. For more details, see *Comprehensive Peace Agreement between the Government of Liberia and the Liberians United for Reconciliation and Democracy (LURD) and the Movement for Democracy in Liberia (MODEL) and Political Parties*. 2003. Available online at: http://www.usip.org/files/file/resources/collections/peace_agreements/liberia_08182003.pdf (Accessed on 23 July 2011).

[52] The mission was authorized by UNSCR 1497. Its mandate was later defined by UNSCR 1509. See United Nations Security Council (UNSC). *Resolution 1497 (2003)*. New York, 2003. Available online at: http://daccess-dds-ny.un.org/doc/UNDOC/GEN/N03/449/48/PDF/N0344948.pdf?OpenElement (Accessed on 19 July 2011); United Nations Security Council (UNSC). *Resolution 1509 (2003)*. New York, 2003. Available online at: http://www.un.org/ga/search/view_doc.asp?symbol=S/RES/1509%282003%29 (Accessed on 19 July 2011).

[53] World Bank. *Data and Statistics* [Website]. 2011. Available online at: http://web.worldbank.org/WBSITE/EXTERNAL/COUNTRIES/AFRICAEXT/LIBERIAEXTN/0,,menuPK:356220~pagePK:141132~piPK:141109~theSitePK:356194,00.html (Accessed on 27 August 2011).

0.766, which indicates that women are strongly discriminated against.[54] The unemployment rate is 75 per cent. 80 per cent of the population lives below the poverty line, 55 per cent even in extreme poverty.[55] Many problems such as the insufficient infrastructure and the poor educational system were exacerbated by the wars and continue to have repercussions. In terms of security, the country's situation remains fragile.[56]

In sum, this chapter has given an overview of the historical and socio-cultural background, including relevant aspects of the gender order, to the Liberian conflict as well as its course. In the subsequent chapter, the impact of the conflict on gender relations and Liberian women's roles in the conflict will be analysed from a gender perspective.

---

[54] This shows that there is great gender inequality, as the gender inequality index ranges from 0 (equality) to 1 (strong inequality). United Nations Development Programme (UNDP). *Human Development Report 2010: The Real Wealth of Nations: Pathways to Human Development.* New York, 2010, pp. 145, 159. Available online at: http://hdr. undp.org/en/reports/global/hdr2010/chapters/ (Accessed on 23 August 2012).

[55] African Women and Peace Support Group. op. cit., p. 6; Fischer Weltalmanach 2008. op. cit., pp. 309.

[56] UNDP. op. cit., *Liberia: Country Profile*; USAID. op. cit., *Liberia: Country Profile*.

4. Liberian women's role in the conflict, peacemaking, peacebuilding and post-conflict reconstruction

Women were both adversely affected by the conflict and participated actively in it. But remarkably, they also engaged in peacemaking and peacebuilding activities as well as post-war reconstruction. Hence, firstly this chapter discusses the impact of the conflict on the female population. Secondly, the commitment and influence of Liberian women's organisations in the creation of peace are examined. Finally, their activities are analysed and evaluated using the analytical framework developed for this objective.[57]

4.1. Gendered implications of the conflict and the participation of women

Internal conflicts, which are the most occurring form of conflicts today, have highly gender-specific repercussions.[58] Compared to inter-state wars, they claim more civilian victims, which are predominantly women and children. Females risk being systematically and strategically targeted by sexual or gender-based violence that is used as a weapon of war in conflicts throughout the world.[59] However, women also assume active roles in conflict settings

---

[57] See Appendix II.

[58] Harders, Cilja. 'Krieg und Frieden in internationalen Beziehungen'. In: Rosenberger, Sieglinde & Sauer, Birgit (eds.). *Politikwissenschaft und Geschlecht. Konzepte – Verknüpfungen – Perspektiven.* Wien, Facultas Verlag, 2004, p. 231; United Nations Women. *Women, War and Peace* [Website]. Undated. Available online at: http://www. womenwarpeace.org/ (Accessed on 25 August 2011).

[59] Aisha, Fatoumata. 'Mainstreaming Gender in Peace Support Operations: The United Nations Mission in Liberia'. In: Aboagye, Festus & Bah, Alahji (eds.). *A Tortuous Road to Peace: The Dynamics of Regional, UN and International Humanitarian Interventions in Liberia.* Pretoria, Publications of the Institute of Security Studies, 2005, p. 148; Kumar, Krishna. 'Civil Wars, Women and Gender Relations: An Overview'. In: ibid. (ed.). *Women and Civil War: Impact, Organizations and Action.* Boulder, Lynne Rienner, 2001, p. 6; Pankhurst, Donna. 'Introduction: Gendered War and Peace'. In: ibid. (ed.). *Gendered Peace: Women's Struggles for Post-War Justice and Reconciliation.* London, Routledge, 2008, pp. 1-3; Pankhurst, Donna. 'Sexual Violence in War'. In: Shepherd, Laura J. (ed.). *Gender Matters in Global Politics. A Feminist Introduction to International Relations.* Abingdon, Routledge, 2010, p. 152.

which highlights the need to look beyond the perception of women as victims, and focus on female agency, too.

Fourteen years of conflict had a devastating effect on Liberia and the Liberian population. It is estimated that up to 250,000 people died. 50 to 75 per cent of the Liberian population, i.e. approximately 2.5 million people, fled to neighbouring and Western countries or became internally displaced persons (IDPs).[60] In both wars, IDPs were particularly affected by the humanitarian crises and subjected to human right abuses and crimes against humanity.[61] For the majority of civilian deaths, refugees and IDPs are females and children, they suffered disproportionally from the violent conflict.[62] Atrocities and breaches of women's – and girls' – rights were committed by all conflict parties on a large scale. These included, rape and other forms of sexual violence, torture, abduction, slavery and forced marriage or forced recruitment. Women were also indirectly affected as the fighting destroyed infrastructures, among others public services, utilities and the economy, leaving them with augmenting rates of illiteracy, unemployment and thus poverty.[63] The extreme

---

[60] Aisha, Fatoumata. op. cit., p. 147; African Women and Peace Support Group. *Liberian Women Peacemakers: Fighting for the Right to Be Seen, Heard, and Counted*. Trenton, Africa World Press, 2004, pp. 2, 4; United Nations High Commissioner for Refugees (UNHCR). *2003 UNHCR Statistical Yearbook: Country Data Sheet – Liberia*. Geneva, 2005. Available online at: http://www.unhcr.org/41d2c182c.html (Accessed on 27 August 2011), p. 223; Fuest, Veronika. "This Is the Time to Get in Front': Changing Roles and Opportunities for Women in Liberia'. In: *African Affairs*, Vol. 107, No. 427, 2008, p. 205; Yacob-Haliso, Olajumoke. 'If I Could Speak to Madam President: Returnee Women's Experiences of Return, Reintegration and Peace in Liberia'. In: *Liberian Studies Journal*, Vol. 33, No. 1, 2008, p. 3.

[61] Aisha, Fatoumata. op. cit., p. 147.

[62] African Women and Peace Support Group. op. cit., p. 4; Yacob-Haliso, Olajumoke. op. cit., p. 3.

[63] Aboagye, Festus B. & Bah, Alhaji M. S. *Liberia at a Crossroads: A Preliminary Look at the United Nations Mission in Liberia (UNMIL) and the Protection of Civilians*. Pretoria, Institute of Security Studies (Occasional Paper No. 95), 2004. Available online at: http://www.iss.org.za/pubs/papers/95/Paper95.htm (Accessed on 28 June 2011); Aisha, Fatoumata. op. cit., pp. 147, 150; Association of Female Lawyers of Liberia (AFELL) & The Editors. 'Hundreds of Victims Silently Grieving'. In: Turshen, Meredeth & Twagiramariya, Clotilde (eds.). *What Women Do in Wartime*. London, Zed Books, 1998, pp. 130-131, 134; British Broadcasting Corporation (BBC). *Liberia Country Profile* [Website]. 2010. Available online at: http://news.bbc.co.uk/1/hi/world/africa/country_profiles/1043500.stm (Accessed on 25 June 2011); Bennett, Olivia et al. (eds.). *Arms to Fight, Arms to Protect: Women Speak out about Conflict*. London, Panos, 1995, pp. 33, 35-36; Fuest, Veronika. op. cit., p. 205; Gerdes, Felix. *Liberia* [Website]. Arbeitsgemeinschaft Kriegsursachenforschung, Hamburg. http://www.

violence against civilians and the widespread destruction of Liberia also had long-term effects and created a vicious circle. In terms of health, rape victims were affected by (teenage) pregnancies, an increase of HIV/AIDS, stigmatisation and other physical or mental health problems including traumatisation.[64] Likewise, there was no adequate health care available which among other things led to one of the highest maternal mortality rates in the world.[65] Living conditions deteriorated, basic needs, e.g. food, clothing and shelter, were not covered and support structures were lacking, so that women became even more vulnerable to sexual violence, harassment or other forms of abuse and were often forced to provide sexual services in order to survive or protect dependants.[66]

In terms of labour division, women could gain economic independence by leading small businesses or acquiring new skills. In the absence of men during and after the conflict, women expanded their social and economic activities by adopting new and often traditionally male roles including trading, breadwinning and protective roles within their families.[67] This at first sight positive tendency must be seen in a differentiated way. The workload of affected women increased, while they suffered from a deterioration of living conditions if households became female-headed.[68] Female employees in the formal economy were hit by the high unemployment rate after the war.[69]

---

sozialwiss.uni-hamburg.de/publish/lpw/Akuf/kriege/260ak_liberia.htm (Accessed on 05 June 2011).

[64] Aisha, Fatoumata. op. cit., p. 150.

[65] ibid., pp. 147, 150-151; Government of Liberia, United Nations Liberia. *Factsheet: Empowering Women in Liberia: Joint Programme on Gender Equality and Women's Empowerment*. Undated. Available online at: http://www.unliberia.org/doc/genderemail.pdf (Accessed on 17 August 2011).

[66] African Women and Peace Support Group. op. cit., pp. 6-7; Aisha, Fatoumata. op. cit., pp. 147, 150 AFELL & The Editors. op. cit., p. 132; Bennett, Olivia et al. (eds.). op. cit., pp. 36-37; Yacob-Haliso, Olajumoke. op. cit., p. 3.

[67] Fuest, Veronika. op. cit., pp. 209, 211-212. Before the war, trading activities by women were restricted as trade was mainly undertaken by the Mandingos.

[68] African Women and Peace Support Group. op. cit., pp. 7, 9; Aisha, Fatoumata. op. cit., pp. 148-149; AFELL & The Editors. op. cit., pp. 129-137; Badmus, Alani. 'Explaining Women's Roles in the West African Tragic Triplet: Sierra Leone, Liberia, and Cote d'Ivoire in Comparative Perspective'. In: *Journal of Alternative Perspectives in the Social Sciences*, Vol. 1, No. 3, 2009, pp. 808-839; Barnes, Elisabeth. *Agents for Change: Civil Society Roles in Preventing War & Building Peace*. Den Haag, European Centre for Conflict Prevention, International Secretariat of the Global Partnership for the Prevention of Armed Conflict (Issue Paper 2), 2006. Available online at: http://www.gppac.net/documents/GPPAC/Research/Issue_papers_2006_-_2007_/2_Agents_

On balance, age, status and location of individual women determined, whether women gained or lost from the war in economic and professional terms.[70] Opportunities for the already "less educated, marginalised and young women",[71] who are in the majority in (rural) Liberia did not improve, but their precarious economic situation was further aggravated.

However, it is important to recognise that a considerable percentage of women also played very active roles during the civil wars. It is estimated that women and girl fighters represented 30 to 40 per cent of all combatants, totalling 25 to 30 thousand. The majority of these were adult women, whereas the proportion of girl combatants is approximately two per cent. The proportion of female fighters in the Liberian conflict is therefore one of the highest in the world. Women and girls did not only participate by carrying weapons, but supported the factions in many (non-)military ways, e.g. by cooking, farming, carrying goods, spying or as sex slaves and wives.[72] Here, one has to note

---

for_Change.pdf (Accessed on 02 May 2011), pp. 44-45; Bennett, Olivia et al. (eds.). op. cit., pp. 28, 45; Cleaver, Gerry & Massey, Simon. 'Liberia: A Durable Peace at Last?' In: Furley, Oliver & May, Roy (eds.). *Ending Africa's Wars. Progressing to Peace.* Aldershot, Ashgate, 2006, pp. 197-199; Fleshman, Michael. 'African Women Struggle for a Seat at the Peace Table'. In: *Africa Renewal* [Website], Vol., 16, No. 4, 2003. Available online at: http://www.un.org/ecosocdev/geninfo/afrec/vol16no4/164wm1.htm (Accessed on 23 April 2011); Fuest, Veronika. op. cit., pp. 209, 211-212; Pedersen, Jennifer. 'In the Rain and in the Sun: Women in Peacebuilding in Liberia'. International Studies Association Annual Convention on *Bridging Multiple Divides.* San Francisco, 26-29 March 2008. Available online at: http://www.allacademic.com//meta/p_mla_apa_research_citation/2/5/3/1/3/pages253135/p253135-1.php (Accessed on 25 April 2011); Solomon, Christiana. 'The Mano River Union Sub-region: The Role of Women in Building Peace'. In: Baksh, Rawwida et al. (eds.). *Gender Mainstreaming in Conflict Transformation: Building Sustainable Peace.* London, Commonwealth Secretariat, 2005, pp. 171-180.

[69] Aisha, Fatoumata. op. cit., p. 149.
[70] Fuest, Veronika. op. cit., pp. 208-209.
[71] ibid., p. 223.
[72] Aisha, Fatoumata. op. cit., pp. 148-149; Amnesty International (AI). *Liberia: A Flawed Process Discriminates against Women and Girls.* 2008, pp. 5, 48. Available online at: http://www.amnesty.org/en/library/asset/AFR34/004/2008/en/c075d220-00cf-11dd-a9d5-b31ac3ea5bcc/afr340042008eng.pdf (Accessed on 04 July 2011); Amnesty International (AI). *Lessons from Liberia: Reintegrating Women in Postconflict Liberia.* 2009, p. 1. Available online at: http://www.amnesty.org/en/library/asset/AFR34/002/2009/en/442e0181-c8e2-4057-81f6-d19ceddf0045/afr340022009en.pdf (Accessed on 28 June 2011); Bennett, Olivia et al. (eds.). op. cit., pp. 33, 38, 48.

that the distinction between agency and victimhood is often flawed.[73] Some women chose to participate in the fighting in order

> "to protect themselves from sexual violence, to avenge the death of family members, because of peer pressure, for material gain, and for survival."[74]

It is also argued, that both young women and men volunteered in order to find marrying partners, while many others were abducted or forced to join conflict parties or lacked alternatives.[75]

Difficulties of female combatants did not cease with the end of the fighting. This is due to the fact that the Liberian disarmament, demobilisation, reintegration and rehabilitation efforts (DDRR)[76] did not adequately consider and provide for women's needs, but they were even discriminated against and suffered from the consequences. Besides, they faced stigmatisation and marginalisation when they returned to their communities, which further worsened their already problematic situation.[77]

All in all, Liberian women experienced the conflict differently depending on factors such as age, ethnicity or origin, which influenced their roles as victims or agents in the conflict. In the following section, another important aspect of women's agency – their struggle for peace – will be discussed.

---

[73] For example, women and girls were forced to join armed groups and to provide sexual services. Aisha, Fatoumata. op. cit., p. 147; AI. op. cit., *Liberia: A Flawed Process,* p. 5.

[74] AI. op. cit., *Liberia: A Flawed Process,* p. 5.

[75] Aisha, Fatoumata. op. cit., pp. 148-149; AI. op. cit., *Lessons from Liberia,* p. 1; AI. op. cit., *Liberia: A Flawed Process,* pp. 11-14; Bennett, Olivia et al. (eds.). op. cit., pp. 6, 9-11, 39, 48; Fuest, Veronika. op. cit., p. 210; Richards, Paul. 'Young Men and Gender in War and Postwar Reconstruction: Some Comparative Findings from Liberia and Sierra Leone. In: Bannon, Ian & Correia, Maria C. (eds.). *The Other Half of Gender: Men's Issues in Development.* Washington D.C., The World Bank, 2006, pp. 197, 208.

[76] For more information on the DDRR, see AI. op. cit., *Liberia: A Flawed Process;* AI. op. cit., *Lessons from Liberia;* Nilsson, Desirée & Söderberg Kovacs, Mimmi. 'Breaking the Cycle of Violence ? Promises and Pitfalls of the Liberian Peace Process'. In: *Civil Wars,* Vol. 7, No. 4, 2005, p. 405 and section 5.1.

[77] AI. op. cit., *Liberia: A Flawed Process,* pp. 15, 19; Bennett, Olivia et al. (eds.). op. cit., p. 39.

4.2. Informal and formal participation of women: The examples of the Liberian Women's Initiative, the Mano River Union Women Peace Network and the Women in Peacebuilding Network

From 2003, activities of the female peace movement attracted particular international attention. But their commitment already started directly after the outbreak of the first conflict. Due to the huge variety of women's groups and movements,[78] the study will focus on three major organisations here, the Liberian Women's Initiative (LWI), the Mano River Union Women Peace Network (MARWOPNET) and the Women in Peacebuilding Network (WIPNET). They are selected because they operated on the grassroots level as well as on a large scale, including even the national and sub-regional political level, and because their activities are sufficiently recorded.[79]

Women's organisations were already active during the first civil war undertaking relief activities.[80] In February 1994, the non-partisan, class transcending Liberian Women's Initiative was founded. It worked for peace with the help of activities such as publishing position statements, meetings, praying, demonstrations, "stay-home actions" and other publicly effective activities and spoke

---

[78] A detailed analysis of the various women's organisations fighting for peace is beyond the scope of this study. For more information, see African Women and Peace Support Group. op. cit.

[79] A broad body of literature about Liberian women's participation in the peace process was identified, for example African Women and Peace Support Group. op. cit.; Disney, Abigail E. & Reticker, Gini (dirs.). *Pray the Devil Back to Hell* [DVD Documentary]. New York, Fork Films, 2008; Ekiyor, Thelma Aremiebi & Gbowee, Leymah Roberta. *Women's Peace Activism in West Africa: The WIPNET Experience* [Website]. 2005. Available online at: http://www.peoplebuildingpeace.org/thestories/article.php?id=80&typ=theme&pid=18 (Accessed on 27 April 2011); George, Kla Emmanuel Gamoe. *Women as Agents of Peace During the Civil Wars in Liberia and Sierra Leone, 1989—2005.* Undated. (Mimeographed Paper). Available online at: www.isud.typepad.com/files/george1.doc (Accessed on 28 April 2011); Great Initiative. *Liberia – Women Bringing Peace to the* Country [Website]. 2011. Available online at: http://www.thegreatinitiative.com/inspiring-story/liberia-mother-brownell/_(Accessed on 06 July 2011); Pedersen, Jennifer. op. cit.; Solomon, Christiana. op, cit., pp. 171-180; Svensson, Katja. 'Women Hold up Half the Sky: Peace and Security Lessons from Liberia'. In: *African Security Review,* Vol. 17, No. 4, 2008, pp. 178-183; 'Women of Liberia's Mass Action for Peace'. In: *The Scavenger: Salvaging What's Left after the Masses Have Had Their Feed.* Undated. Available online at: http://www.thescavenger.net/people/women-of-liberias-mass-action-for-peace-37462-315.html (Accessed on 07 June 2012).

[80] African Women and Peace Support Group. op. cit., pp. ix-xiii.

out in favour of disarmament and its effective implementation. At the end of the year, LWI delegates participated in peace meetings of the ECOWAS in Ghana. Although initially not invited, they became observers and finally obtained official recognition. A similar scenario happened 1995 in Abuja, where women from the LWI, despite initial scepticism by the participants of the peace talks,[81] presented a factual paper revealing the catastrophic humanitarian situation and the suffering of civilians to the sub-regional heads of state, which is considered to have helped achieve progress in the negotiations. By this action, not only did women exert influence on the sub-regional organisation and other external actors, but interacted with rebel groups whose cooperation was necessary to reach a sustainable agreement supported by all warring factions. After the cessation of hostilities, the LWI organised civic and voter education initiatives as well as workshops on non-violence, conflict resolution and encouraged women to participate in the post-conflict reconstruction. All in all, the initiative undertook various sustainable activities for peace.[82]

Furthermore, it should be remembered that already at this time, women were present at the state level as the examples of Ruth Perry, head of the Council of the State of the 1993 interim government, who opposed warlords in order to reach peace, and Ellen Johnson-Sirleaf, who challenged Charles Taylor in the presidential elections in 1997 and finished second, show.[83]

---

[81] ibid., pp. 26-27, 76-77.

[82] The information concerning the activities of the LWI is taken from the following sources: African Women and Peace Support Group. op. cit., pp. ix-xiii, 8-16, 18, 20-27, 31, 41-43; AFELL & The Editors. op. cit., p. 133; Conciliation Resources. *Accord Liberia Project* [Website]. 2011. Available online at: http://www.c-r.org/our-work/accord/liberia/index.php (Accessed on 08 July 2011); Fleshman, Michael. op. cit.; Ghana Center for Democratic Development. *Liberian Women's Initiative, LWI - Liberia (local)* [Website]. 2011. Available online at: http://www.cddghana.org/ngod.asp?ng=44htm (Accessed on 06 July 2011); Great Initiative. *Liberia – Women Bringing Peace to the Country* [Website]. 2011. Available online at: http://www.thegreatinitiative.com/inspiring-story/liberia-mother-brownell/ (Accessed on 06 July 2011); Peacebuilding Portal. *Liberian Women's Initiative (LWI)* [Website]. 2011. Available online at: http://www.peacebuildingportal.org/index.asp?pgid=9&org=2827 (Accessed on 07 July 2011); Solomon, Christiana. op. cit., p. 177.

[83] African Women and Peace Support Group. op. cit., pp. 30-31; AFELL & The Editors. op. cit., p. 134; Fuest, Veronika. op. cit., p. 214

In May 2000, during the second civil war, the Mano River Union Women Peace Network, a regional women's organisation was created with the support of ECOWAS and other (non-)governmental organisations. It comprised women from Liberia, Sierra Leone and Guinea. They fought together for peace, disarmament and conflict prevention in the Mano River Union[84] as well as the participation of women in decision-making concerning issues of peace and security. The organisation adopted a multilevel approach including activities on the community and grassroots level, as well as consultations and contacts with national, sub-regional, regional and international actors. When the initiative successfully brought the Liberian, Sierra Leonean and Guinean presidents together to negotiate peace in 2001, it was simultaneously a great achievement and failure: MARWOPNET itself could not participate in the talks due to their political marginalisation and lack of resources. However, two years later, the organisation officially co-mediated and signed the Liberian peace agreement. In 2003, it was awarded the UN Prize in the Field of Human Rights.[85]

While LWI and MARWOPNET continued their activities, a new women's movement emerged in 2001, when the West Africa Network for Peacebuilding (WANEP) initiated the Women in Peacebuilding Network (WIPNET) in order

"to elevate women from their state of obscurity to the fore to enable them play key roles alongside men in building peace".[86]

This group comprised women of different religious affiliations, i.e. Christians and Muslims, social class, ethnicities and age groups, who had differing ex-

---

[84] The Mano River Union comprises Liberia, Sierra Leone and Guinea.
[85] African Women and Peace Support Group. op. cit., pp. ix-xiii, 39-46; Fleshman, Michael. op. cit.; Mano River Union Women Peace Network (MARWOPNET). *MARWOPNET Liberia Country Report: December 2001-December 2003*. Undated. Available online at: http://www.marwopnet.org/liberia_activies.pdf (Accessed on 09 July 2011); *Réseau des Femmes du Fleuve Mano pour la Paix (REFMAP)* [Website]. 2009. Available online at: http://www.marwopnet.org/index.html (Accessed on 09 July 2011); Solomon, Christiana. op. cit., pp. 178; United Nations (UN). *United Nations Prize in the Field of Human Rights: 2003 Awardees* [Website]. Undated. Available online at: http://www.un.org/events/humanrights/2003/awards.html (Accessed on 09 July 2011).
[86] Global Network of Women Peacebuilders (GNWP). *WIPNET* [Website]. Available online at: http://www.gnwp.org/members/wipnet (Accessed on 19 July 2011).

periences of the conflict but who were all united by the desire for peace.[87] So in 2002, the Liberian Mass Action for Peace was born, which had a substantial role in the final phase of the Liberian conflict. The women involved took their protest against the war to the streets: Every morning, dressed in white, they assembled in a strategic place in Monrovia – and other locations throughout the country – with their placards. Soon, over 2,500 women with different social backgrounds participated in the sitting, dancing, singing, weeping, praying and fasting for peace in the capital.[88] They were eventually allowed to meet President Taylor to present their position statement urging peace talks between the warring factions. Besides, they exerted pressure by establishing contacts with different stakeholders such as the rebels and the US.[89] Finally, the conflict parties agreed to meet. This allowed for the beginning of the peace talks in Ghana that were organized by the ECOWAS. WIPNET itself was not initially invited to the meeting, but fund-raising activities within Liberia enabled a delegation to travel to the venue, whose members were then supported by Liberian refugee women living in Ghana. The negotiations were protracted, while the situation in Liberia, especially Monrovia, deteriorated. When no outcome was achieved, the WIPNET and refugee women present in Ghana blocked the doors with a sit-in, forcing the parties to finally come to an agreement, the Comprehensive Peace Agreement.[90]

The activities of Liberian women continued after the signing of the accord. In December 2003, the UN started their disarmament, demobilisation, reintegration and rehabilitation programme together with the Liberian transitional government. Despite attempts by members of women's organisations to partici-

---

[87] Disney, Abigail E. & Reticker, Gini (dirs.). op. cit.; Hack, Nadine B. 'Liberia: Women's Mass Action for Peace and 'Pray the Devil Back to Hell' Screening at Samuel K Doe Stadium'. In: *AllAfrica*. 9 March, 2009. Available online at: http://allafrica.com/stories/200903170823.html (Accessed on 08 July 2011); MARWOPNET. op. cit.; Sawyer, Amos. 'Emerging Patterns in Liberia's Post-Conflict Politics: Observations from the 2005 Elections'. In: *African Affairs*, Vol. 107, No. 427, 2008, p. 188; 'Women of Liberia's Mass Action for Peace'. op. cit.

[88] African Women and Peace Support Group. op. cit., pp. 46-48; Disney, Abigail E. & Reticker, Gini (dirs.). op. cit. Women from different social class, ethnicity and of various ages were mobilised to participate in activities organized by women's organisations.

[89] Disney, Abigail E. & Reticker, Gini (dirs.). op. cit.

[90] African Women and Peace Support Group. op. cit., pp. 46-48; Disney, Abigail E. & Reticker, Gini (dirs.). op. cit.; 'Women of Liberia's Mass Action for Peace'. op. cit.

pate and to contribute their experience of former DDRR activities, the UN first refused their involvement and agreed only later, when the process caused problems.[91] Then, women helped by undertaking measures aiming at reconciliation, re-humanisation and re-establishing relations. For example, women's organisations convinced ex-combatants to participate in DDRR and helped to re-integrate child soldiers in their communities.[92] Other peacebuilding activities consisted in the destruction of small arms and light weapons (SALW), support for refugees and IDPs, promotion of non-violent conflict transformation within communities, awareness rising and workshops on issues related to gender or peace etc.[93]

In 2005, before the presidential elections, female activists successfully raised awareness regarding the importance of political participation, encouraged women's voter registration and undertook educational activities. Many women registered, consequently, increasing their total share of the electorate to approximately 50 per cent. They also campaigned for Ellen Johnson-Sirleaf, a Harvard-educated economist and politician.[94] In November 2005, she won the presidential elections, which consist of two rounds of direct majority voting.[95] Several factors contributed to her victory, which will be discussed in the following chapter (see 5.2.). However, it is noteworthy in this context that she succeeded mainly thanks to the votes of the educated urban elite and wom-

---

[91] For more information on the difficulties of the DDRR process, see Al. op. cit., *Liberia: A Flawed Process*; International Crisis Group (ICG). *Liberia: Uneven Progress in Security Sector Reform*. Africa Report No. 148, 2009, pp. 27-30. Available online at: http://www.crisisgroup.org/en/regions/africa/west-africa/liberia/148-liberia-uneven-progress-in-security-sector-reform.aspx (Accessed on 20 July 2011).

[92] 'Women of Liberia's Mass Action for Peace'. op. cit.

[93] Disney, Abigail E. & Reticker, Gini (dirs.). op. cit.; Jones, Katelyn. 'West African Women Unite: The Inclusion of Women in Peace Processes'. In: *Undergraduate Transitional Justice Review*, Vol. 1, No. 2, 2011, pp. 167; 'Women of Liberia's Mass Action for Peace'. op. cit.; *REFMAP*. op. cit.; West Africa Network for Peacebuilding (WANEP). *Rapport Annuel 2009*. Accra, WANEP, 2009, pp. 13, 20. Available online at: http://www.wanep.org/wanep/attachments/article/202/ar_2009_fr.pdf (Accessed on 20 August 2011).

[94] For a more detailed biography of Ellen Johnson-Sirleaf, see chapter 5.1.

[95] The Liberian political system is largely identical with the US-American one, although it is not federal. The Liberian president is elected directly. *Constitution of the Republic of Liberia*. 1986, art. 83b. Available online at: http://confinder.richmond.edu/admin/docs/liberia.pdf (Accessed on 21 July 2011). For a profound analysis of the election results, see Sawyer, Amos. op. cit.

en, although it is unclear if the support of the latter was disproportional and that the way to her election was partly paved by the previous existence and activities of the women's movement.[96]

The election of a female head of state and government is often seen as the climax of Liberian women's efforts, as a woman is formally represented on the state level and is assumed to progress women's issues.[97] However, although achievements were certainly brought about, the variety of persistent challenges that the women's movement faced should not be ignored. Hence, in the following section, the factors that led to positive outcomes or limited successes are assessed.

4.3. Achievements, problems and missed opportunities: Critical review of women's activities in the settlement of the Liberian conflict

The chronology of the Liberian women's peace movement is admirable. But achievements as well as potential difficulties must be evaluated qualitatively in order to find out, what – if anything – they accomplished. Thus, in the first part of this section, the positive effects are analysed qualitatively. The second part focuses on the problems the women faced.

It is true that Liberian women contributed to the making and building of peace, among others by organising demonstrations, lobbying factional leaders and supporting DDRR.[98] They established contacts between different stakeholders, including external ones, and engaged in mediation. In so doing, they attained progress that may not have been realised otherwise. For example, both the peace talks in Accra in summer 2003 and the final outcome, the Comprehensive Peace Agreement between the Liberian government and the

---

[96] BBC. op. cit.; Disney, Abigail E. & Reticker, Gini (dirs.). op. cit; Sawyer, Amos. op. cit., p. 198.
[97] Sawyer, Amos op. cit., p. 198.
[98] African Women and Peace Support Group. op. cit., pp. 46-48; Disney, Abigail E. & Reticker, Gini (dirs.). op. cit.; 'Women of Liberia's Mass Action for Peace'. op. cit. See also section 4.2.

rebel factions LURD and MODEL, were only possible thanks to the commitment and pressure of women.[99] They could exert influence because the initiatives were strong, mostly impartial and credible. Besides, they embraced women of different backgrounds and made use of their crucial non-material resources such as personal contacts and their broad network permeating Liberian society at all levels.[100]

Furthermore, it is argued that the participation of women's organisations in the peace process was successful because it did not touch or modify existing social and power relations, which implies that the movements did not relate to "traditional notions of domination",[101] but other channels of influence were used. When women tried to maintain female leadership after the conflict or to progressively transform (male-dominated) structures, e.g. by participating in peace talks, the DDRR or the elections, they immediately faced greater resistance from men who felt that their position was challenged.[102] In addition, activities by women's organisations did not interfere with government politics, but concentrated exclusively on the demand for peace, as otherwise, members would have risked prosecution.[103] The agenda of women's initiatives was thus very pragmatic and restricted, which contributed to their success on the one hand. On the other, the non-inclusion of women's issues in political debates limited their influence concerning these topics to a large degree after the conflict and helps to explain their marginalisation. At the institutional level, the appointment of Ruth Perry as head of the Council of State was a success, as was the election of Ellen Johnson-Sirleaf.

---

[99] African Women and Peace Support Group. op. cit., pp. 42-45; Pillay, Anu. 'Truth Seeking and Gender: The Liberian Experience'. In: *African Journal on Conflict Resolution*, Vol. 9, No. 2, 2009, p. 91. Available online at: http://www.accord.org.za/downloads/ajcr/ajcr_2009_2.pdf?phpMyAdmin=ceeda2df659e6d3e35a63d69e93228f1 (Accessed on 19 July 2011). See also African Women and Peace Support Group. op. cit., pp. 27-29.

[100] African Women and Peace Support Group. op. cit., pp. 17, 34; Disney, Abigail E. & Reticker, Gini (dirs.). op. cit.; 'Women of Liberia's Mass Action for Peace'. op. cit.

[101] 'Women of Liberia's Mass Action for Peace'. op. cit.

[102] See Al. op. cit., *Lessons from Liberia*; 'Women of Liberia's Mass Action for Peace'. op. cit.

[103] Disney, Abigail E. & Reticker, Gini (dirs.). op. cit.

These achievements must be regarded critically though.[104] It remains to be seen if they are not only of a quantitative nature, but bring about little qualitative changes because

> "the election of one woman to a position of authority, particularly when surrounded by men with varying political motivations, could not guarantee the achievement of Liberian women's hopes for peace and reconciliation"[105]

or greater attention for gender issues.[106] Besides, women are not necessarily more gender-sensitive than men and often have to adopt 'masculine' features in order to survive in politics.[107] Thus, it is arguable, if the influence of the women's movement persists due to a female president, as Sawyer claims.[108]

Bouta et al. argue that a major problem of women regarding issues of peace is that they participate more in the informal than the formal process, which is also true in Liberia.[109] In this context,

> "[i]t is crucial [...] that initiatives undertaken outside of political peace negotiations and processes are not stripped of their inherently political meanings, outcomes and impacts".[110]

This highlights that they are certainly politically relevant, but skills obtained in informal processes are not necessarily transferable to formal settings.[111] Although Liberian women's peace movements partly managed the transition from the informal to the formal, they often remained excluded from the decision-making arena and their concerns were marginalised.[112] Furthermore, their participation was especially appreciated and allowed when it helped to advance the deadlocked peace process, but was neglected when this was

---

[104] African Women and Peace Support Group. op. cit., pp. 30-31.
[105] ibid., p. 31.
[106] See African Women and Peace Support Group. op. cit., p. 55; Bekoe, Dorina & Parajon, Christina. *Women's Role in Liberia's Reconstruction* [Website]. Washington D.C., United States Institute for Peace, 2007. Available online at: http://www.usip.org/publicationswomen-s-role-liberia-s-reconstruction (Accessed on 20 August 2011).
[107] Bouta, Tsjeard et al. *Gender, Conflict, and Development*. Washington D.C., The World Bank, 2005, p. 49; Caprioli, Mary & Boyer, Mark A. 'Gender, Violence, and International Crisis'. In: *The Journal of Conflict Resolution*, Vol. 45, No. 4, 2001, pp. 507-508.
[108] Sawyer, Amos. op. cit., p. 188.
[109] See Bouta, Tsjeard et al. op. cit., pp. 49-51, 65-66.
[110] African Women and Peace Support Group. op. cit., p. 34.
[111] Bouta, Tsjeard et al. op. cit., p. 61.
[112] Pillay, Anu. op. cit., 'Truth Seeking and Gender', p. 93; 'Women of Liberia's Mass Action for Peace'. op. cit.

not the case. This suggests that they were to some degree used to advance the process, while their gender needs and interests remained largely ignored.

There were also internal difficulties. Firstly, the initiatives' potential and scope were limited by problems such as funding, training opportunities and capacity building. In financial terms, the organisations received some external support from African and Western NGOs and governments as well as international organisations.[113] However, this was inadequate and – especially in situations where money was urgently needed – the groups covered their expenses autonomously by fundraising.[114] Secondly, although there was some cooperation between different groups, their activities were not properly coordinated. Instead, there was even competition and mistrust due to splits resulting from "[d]iffering political, religious, social and economic affiliations",[115] as well as dissent between groups regarding targets.[116] In both cases, the movements were considerably weakened. Thirdly, some women participating in negotiations represented factional rather than overarching women's ideas. In this case, they had better access to the rebel factions, but it harmed the political neutrality and impartiality of the women's movement. Finally, within women's communities and families there was the fear that their activity could attract retaliation against the whole group, which meant that women faced pressure from their social support networks.[117]

In sum, the movement must be seen in its socio-cultural context. It must not be underestimated, as women acted in a highly dangerous, unsecure environment and often at "personal risk".[118] In Liberia the majority of the female population traditionally possess little or no influence in the public and political sphere. Under these circumstances, its results are considerable. It is possible

---

[113] *REFMAP.* op. cit.
[114] Bekoe, Dorina & Parajon, Christina. op. cit.; *REFMAP.* op. cit.
[115] African Women and Peace Support Group. op. cit., p. 32.
[116] ibid., p. 25; Fleshman, Michael. op. cit.; Solomon, Christiana. op. cit., p. 178-179. See also Kellow, Tim. *Women, Elections and Violence in West Africa: Assessing Women's Political Participation in Liberia and Sierra Leone.* London, International Alert, 2010. Available online at: http://www.international-alert.org/sites/default/files/publications/ 201012WomenElectionsViolenceWestAfrica.pdf (Accessed on 20 July 2011).
[117] African Women and Peace Support Group. op. cit., pp. 23, 32-33.
[118] ibid., p. 12. See also ibid., pp. 22, 32, 34; Disney, Abigail E. & Reticker, Gini (dirs.). op. cit.

that this success in peacebuilding – and the growing recognition of their contribution – will help women to exert greater influence in decision-making in the
future. However, the achievements are not to be overestimated either. It is
more than questionable if the women's movement is really present on the
formal political level thanks to the election of Johnson-Sirleaf, whose work will
be discussed in the following, or if this is not too positive an assessment.[119]
The analysis of post-conflict Liberia, which will follow in the sixth chapter,
highlights that women depending on their socio-economic status continue to
face multiple – although divergent – difficulties.

---

[119] 'Women of Liberia's Mass Action for Peace'. op. cit.

5. Ellen Johnson-Sirleaf's electoral victory: Final success or litmus test for Liberia's women?

It is impossible to study post-conflict Liberia without taking into account the role of Ellen Johnson-Sirleaf who made the headlines several times. By winning the elections in 2005, she became the first elected female president in Africa. In 2011, her name was again on everyone's lips, when she was awarded the Nobel Peace Prize together with Liberian Leymah Gbowee,[1] who coordinated the Women of Liberia Mass Action for Peace, and a Yemenite human rights activist, Tawakkol Karman, "for their non-violent struggle for the safety of women and for women's rights to full participation in peace-building work".[2] Shortly after this, she was re-elected for a second term.[3] But how is Ellen Johnson-Sirleaf's triumph to be interpreted? Is it the logical consequence of more than a decade of women's activism or is it still an unexpected development in Liberian politics? This chapter aims at shedding light on the circumstances under which Africa's first female head of state accessed power and how she performed in office. For this purpose, it is first of all necessary to provide an overview of Johnson-Sirleaf's political biography.[4] After that, her electoral victory will be examined against the broader socio-cultural background. Finally, achievements and pitfalls of her first term in office (2006-2011) will be critically assessed by reference to major political issues.

---

[1] For a detailed overview of her contribution to peacemaking in Liberia, see Disney, Abigail E. & Reticker, Gini (dirs.). *Pray the Devil Back to Hell* [DVD Documentary]. New York, Fork Films, 2008.

[2] Nobel Prize. *The Nobel Peace Prize 2011: Ellen Johnson-Sirleaf, Leymah Gbowee, Tawakkol Karman* [Website]. 2012. Available online at: http://www.nobelprize.org/ nobel_prizes/peace/laureates/2011/johnson_sirleaf.html# (Accessed on 30 May 2012).

[3] Due to their recent nature, the 2011 ballots, i.e. the referendum in August and the elections in autumn will not be taken into consideration here. For a detailed report on the elections, see Carter Center. *Pre-Publication: Final Report National Elections in Liberia.* Atlanta, 2011. Available online at: http://www.cartercenter.org/resources/pdfs/news/ peace_publications/election_reports/liberia2011-finalrpt-pp.pdf (Accessed on 08 May 2012).

[4] For it is beyond the scope of this study to provide an encompassing insight into Ellen Johnson-Sirleaf's biography, only aspects relevant for the analysis will be addressed.

5.1. The political career of the Liberian Iron Lady

Who is this person referred to as "Iron Lady" of Liberia or "Ma Ellen"?[5] Ellen Johnson-Sirleaf was born in 1938 in Monrovia. Her ethnic origin is disputed. She claims to have Gola, Kru and German roots and thus, to be mainly of indigenous origin. However, she is often considered to belong to the Americo-Liberian elite, as her family moved up the social ladder due to work and education: She studied economics at the University of Colorado and Harvard among others.[6] Johnson-Sirleaf has many years of political activity behind her, during which she served and opposed several governments. She was implicated in all phases of Liberia's recent political history. On the one hand, this reveals her political experience and qualification, which is certainly an advantage in the eyes of the international community. On the other, it suggests why her person is controversial especially in her home country.

Although having criticised the government, Johnson-Sirleaf worked for the Department of Treasury and finally served as Minister of Finance (1979-1980) in the True Whig Government of William Tolbert.[7] When Samuel Doe took power in 1980, she narrowly escaped the political purges following his coup, while the majority of the members of the former Cabinet were executed. She led the Liberian Bank for Development and Investment at Doe's request before going into exile to Kenya and the US. In 1985, after having challenged

---

[5] Cantrell, Tania H. & Bachmann, Ingrid. 'Who Is the Lady in the Window? A Comparison of International and National Press Coverage of First Female Government Heads'. In: *Journalism Studies*, Vol. 9, No 3, 2008, pp. 438; Thomas, Gwynn & Adams, Melinda. 'Breaking the Final Glass Ceiling: The Influence of Gender in the Elections of Ellen Johnson-Sirleaf and Michelle Bachelet'. In: *Journal of Women*, Vol. 31, No. 2, 2010, pp. 118, 122.

[6] Benner, Thorsten & Blume, Till. 'A Second Chance for Liberia: President Johnson-Sirleaf's Quest to Build a New Liberia'. In: *Internationale Politik - Global Edition*, No. 9, 2008, p. 41; Dennis, Peter. *A Brief History of Liberia*. New York, The International Center for Transitional Justice, 2006. Available online at: http://ictj.org/sites/default/files/ICTJ-Liberia-Brief-History-2006-English.pdf (Accessed on 07 May 2012); Harris, David. 'Liberia 2005: an Unusual African Post-conflict Election'. In: *Journal of Modern African Studies*, Vol. 44, No. 3, 2006, pp. 384, 390; International Crisis Group (ICG). *Liberia: How Sustainable is the Recovery?* Africa Report No. 177, 2011, p. 5. Available online at: http://www.crisisgroup.org/~/media/Files/africa/west-africa/liberia/177%20Liberia%20-%20How%20Sustainable%20is%20the%20Recovery.pdf (Accessed on 02 May 2012).

[7] Tonpo, Jarlawah. 'Johnson Sirleaf: 'Taylor Fooled Me''. In: *New African*, May, 2009, pp. 41.

Doe in senatorial elections, she was sentenced to ten years imprisonment and had to flee the country again.[8] In the 1997 presidential elections, Ellen Johnson-Sirleaf campaigned against Taylor who won by a 75 per cent landslide victory.[9] After the end of the conflict, she returned to Liberia and became a member of the Governance Reform Commission and chairwoman of the Commission on Good Governance of the transitional government, whose main task consisted in fighting corruption.[10] In addition to her political activities, Johnson-Sirleaf performed different executive functions in the economic and financial sector in Nairobi and Washington and worked among other things for the World Bank and as an Assistant Administrator and later as a Director of the UN Development Program Regional Bureau for Africa (1992-1997).[11]

An especially important and controversial aspect of her political activity is her involvement in Charles Taylor's revolution in 1989 that led to the outbreak of the conflict. Ellen Johnson-Sirleaf is accused and criticised for having morally and financially supported Charles Taylor because she had considered his invasion necessary in order to overthrow Doe's regime and restore democracy. However, her endorsement for his cause ceased in 1990, when she distanced herself from Taylor.[12] Despite her testimony and apologies in front of

---

[8] Cooper, Helene. 'Iron Lady: The Promise of Liberia's Ellen Johnson-Sirleaf'. In: *World Affairs*, November/December, 2010, p. 47; Dennis, Peter. op. cit.; Tonpo, Jarlawah. op. cit., pp. 41-42.

[9] African Election Database. *Elections in Liberia* [Website]. 2011. Available online at: http://africanelections.tripod.com/lr.html#1997_Presidential_Election (Accessed on 04 May 2012). Taylor's electoral victory is largely attributed to the fact that people feared the consequences of his defeat and his control over key resources including the media. Adams, Melinda. 'Liberia's Election of Ellen Johnson-Sirleaf and Women's Executive Leadership in Africa'. In: *Politics & Gender*, Vol. 4, No. 3, 2008, pp. 478-479; Nilsson, Desirée & Söderberg Kovacs, Mimmi. 'Breaking the Cycle of Violence? Promises and Pitfalls of the Liberian Peace Process'. In: *Civil Wars*, Vol. 7, No. 4, 2005, p. 399.

[10] Integrated Regional Information Networks (IRIN). *Liberia: Johnson Sirleaf Rejoins the Political Fray* [Website]. 30 January, 2004. Available online at: http://www.irinnews.org/ Report/48367/LIBERIA-Johnson-Sirleaf-rejoins-the-political-fray (Accessed on 20 April 2012).

[11] Dennis, Peter. op. cit.

[12] Adebajo, Adekeye. op. cit., *Liberia's Civil War*, pp. 59-60; Benner, Thorsten & Blume, Till. op. cit., p. 41; Dennis, Peter. op. cit.; Johnson-Sirleaf, Ellen. *Mein Leben für Liberia: Die erste Präsidentin Afrikas erzählt*. Frankfurt on the Main, Krüger Verlag, 2009, pp. 218-231; Harris, David. op. cit., p. 382; Nilsson, Desirée & Söderberg Kovacs, Mimmi. op. cit., p. 407; Tonpo, Jarlawah. op. cit.

the Truth and Reconciliation Commission (TRC), the issue remains disputed and politicised.[13]

It is certainly imperative to consider and question Johnson-Sirleaf's political career and her role in the late 1980s in particular, as neglecting it would lead to a double standard. Nevertheless, a more nuanced interpretation is required without justifying her action. On the one hand, Johnson-Sirleaf was not the only person of the Liberian elite having initially supported Taylor, who also benefitted from considerable assistance by foreign governments. Furthermore, it is questionable if the degree of violence that followed his invasion was predictable.[14] On the other, it is impossible to talk about her endorsement of Taylor without talking about the former regime of Samuel Doe, as this – together with the fact that her political biography is marked by opposition and criticism of various governments – allows for understanding her positioning as a step against Doe and not in favour of Taylor.

The way the matter is dealt with and in many respects politically exploited illustrates to what extent politics are personalised in Liberia. More generally, Johnson-Sirleaf is by far not the only politician with connections to a former warring faction or implicated in the civil war. Another prominent example is Prince Johnson, former leader of the INPFL and responsible for the killing of Samuel Doe, who is a member of the Senate and ran in the 2011 presidential elections. This highlights that the challenges that the Liberian society has to face in terms of personal continuity, impunity and reconciliation have a much greater extent than the case of Ellen Johnson-Sirleaf suggests.

Overall, Ellen Johnson-Sirleaf's political biography helps to understand why she is supported and criticised at the same time. Due to her political and eco-

---

[13] Tonpo, Jarlawah. op. cit., p. 42; Truth and Reconciliation Commission (TRC). *Volume II: Consolidated Final Report*. Monrovia, 2009, p. 361. Available online at: http://trco fliberia.org/resources/reports/final/volume-two_layout-1.pdf (Accessed on 20 April 2012). In its final report, the TRC recommended banning her from office for 30 years as a consequence of her contacts to one of the warring factions and implication in the civil war.

[14] Adebajo, Adekeye. op. cit., *Liberia's Civil War*, pp. 59-60; Nilsson, Desirée & Söderberg Kovacs, Mimmi. op. cit., p. 398; Tonpo, Jarlawah. op. cit., p. 42.

nomic experience and know-how, she has earned international credibility.[15] At the same time, this very experience and the continuity that derives from it can also be problematic, as she is part of the old Liberian elite that is responsible for decades of economic and political mismanagement, whose persistence risks obstructing the emergence of a new leading class that breaks with the past and promotes democratic consolidation.[16]

5.2. Electoral victory with and against a political system

In 2005, presidential elections were held in Liberia in order to replace the transitional government by an elected administration.[17] In the first round, none of the candidates obtained the absolute majority required by the constitution.[18] Hence, a run-off was organised, in which Ellen Johnson-Sirleaf obtained 59.4 per cent of the votes and outpolled her challenger ex-footballer George Manne Weah.[19] The electoral process was considered free and fair as well as generally successful due to the low level of violence; however, turnout was not over-average.[20] In January 2006, Ellen Johnson-Sirleaf was inaugurated and became the first publicly elected female head of state in Africa. But is her success the logical consequence of the activity of women's movements and their final breakthrough? Although women's commitment for peace favoured her victory to some extent, such an interpretation is too sim-

---

[15] Ibid., p. 407; IRIN. op. cit., *Liberia: Johnson Sirleaf Rejoins the Political Fray.* See also section 5.3.
[16] Nilsson, Desirée & Söderberg Kovacs, Mimmi. op. cit., p. 407.
[17] For a detailed overview of both presidential and legislative elections, see Harris, David. op. cit.
[18] According to the constitution, all elections consist of two rounds of direct majority voting. *Constitution of the Republic of Liberia.* 1986, art. 83b. Available online at: http://confinder.richmond.edu/admin/docs/liberia.pdf (Accessed on 21 July 2011).
[19] African Election Database. op. cit. Weah claimed that the elections were fraudulent. Integrated Regional Information Networks (IRIN). *Liberia: "Humbled" Ellen Johnson-Sirleaf Confirmed Africa's First Female President* [Website]. 23 November, 2005. Available online at: http://www.irinnews.org/Report/57300/LIBERIA-Humbled-Ellen-Johnson-Sirleaf-confirmed-Africa-s-first-female-president (Accessed on 07 May 2012).
[20] African Election Database. op. cit.; Harris, David. op. cit., pp. 378, 380, 391; IRIN. Op. cit., *Liberia: "Humbled"*; Nilsson, Desirée & Söderberg Kovacs, Mimmi. op. cit., p. 406. The turnout in the first round amounted to 74.9 per cent, in the run off it dropped to 61 per cent. In post-conflict elections in Mozambique or Angola, it amounted to 88 and 91 per cent, respectively. Harris, David. op. cit., p. 380.

plistic. Thus, her election will be examined against the broader socio-cultural background, which helps to identify various factors that both fostered and obstructed her access to power.

Given the discrimination the majority of Liberian women face in various domains of the public and private sphere and given structural, cultural and institutional factors impeding their access to decision-making positions, Ellen Johnson-Sirleaf's election is surprising.[21] Among structural obstacles to women's participation in politics are their insufficient education, economic marginalisation or poverty and labour division resulting in a double-burden for women due to responsibilities in the household and regarding child-rearing.[22] These factors restrict women's capacities and both material and immaterial resources; they make their access to power generally difficult and lead to their underrepresentation in politics. This is further reinforced by cultural beliefs such as gendered stereotypes that prevent women from running for office. For example, politics are perceived as male domain.[23] Furthermore, certain policies such as economics, foreign policy or defence are seen as traditionally male, whereas education or health care are rather women's domains.[24] As the former are of greater relevance in presidential elections, such cultural conceptions can disadvantage female politicians who seem to be insufficiently qualified. Notwithstanding, well-educated individuals can obtain influential positions as the example of Johnson-Sirleaf but also the occasional presence of Americo-Liberian women in pre-war politics highlight. Moreover, gendered beliefs can be overcome and even be instrumentalised in particular circumstances as will be shown later.

---

[21] Thomas, Gwynn & Adams, Melinda. op. cit., pp. 109-113. See also chapter 3.2. and 6.2.

[22] Ibid., pp. 110, 114.

[23] Jalalzai, Farida & Krook, Mona Lena. 'Beyond Hillary and Benazir: Women's Political Leadership Worldwide'. In: *International Political Science Review*, Vol. 31, No. 1, 2010, pp. 6, 11; Jones-Demen, Annie. 'Dynamics of Gender Relations in War-time and Post-war Liberia: Implications for Public Policy'. In: Omeje, Kenneth (ed.). *War to Peace Transition: Conflict Intervention and Peacebuilding in Liberia*. Lanham, University Press of America, 2009, pp. 100, 103; Ogunsanya, Kemi. 'Qualifying Women's Leadership in Africa'. In: *Conflict Trends*, No. 2, 2007, p. 50; Thomas, Gwynn & Adams, Melinda. op. cit., pp. 110-111.

[24] Cantrell, Tania H. & Bachmann, Ingrid. op. cit. pp. 430-431; Thomas, Gwynn & Adams, Melinda. op. cit., p. 120.

In addition, institutional factors such as the nature of the political or the electoral system represent a hurdle for women.[25] In general, women are more likely to access power in parliamentary systems than in presidential regimes. This might be due to the very nature of the different posts and the fact that the distinct functional logics of the systems require distinctive leadership qualities.[26] Furthermore, not only are women more likely to be appointed to an office than to be elected, but there are also differences between different voting systems. Proportional representation is more favourable to women compared to first-past-the-post systems.[27] Finally, women's candidacies are impeded by highly personalised and weakly institutionalised party structures.[28] Hence, the Liberian political system, where the president is selected in a two round system from a great number of competitors – in 2005, there were 22 candidates in the first round – and where parties are strongly personalised is not conducive to women's access to political offices. In addition, other than powerful women in Asia or Latin America, Johnson-Sirleaf did not have connections to a politically influential family or husband that provided her with contacts and support in the political arena.[29] However, there were situation-related circumstances such as the absence of an incumbent or an influential former warlord that led to an opening of the political space and favoured Johnson-Sirleaf's electoral success.[30]

---

[25] A detailed analysis of institutional variables and their functioning can be found in Jalalzai, Farida & Krook, Mona Lena. op. cit.

[26] Jalalzai, Farida & Krook, Mona Lena. op. cit., pp. 9-10, 12; Thomas, Gwynn & Adams, Melinda. op. cit., p. 107. According to Jalazai and Krook, only 13 per cent of female leaders were elected by public vote. Jalalzai, Farida & Krook, Mona Lena. op. cit., p. 12.

[27] Jalalzai, Farida & Krook, Mona Lena. op. cit., pp. 9-10; Thomas, Gwynn & Adams, Melinda. op. cit., p. 110. Women's representation can also be institutionally fostered by quotas, which is, however, irrelevant in the context of presidential elections. Jalalzai, Farida & Krook, Mona Lena. op. cit., pp. 11, 15-17; Ogunsanya, Kemi. op. cit., p. 51

[28] Nilsson, Desirée & Söderberg Kovacs, Mimmi. op. cit., p. 406; Thomas, Gwynn & Adams, Melinda. op. cit., pp. 110, 114.

[29] Adams, Melinda. op. cit., p. 477; Jalalzai, Farida & Krook, Mona Lena. op. cit., p. 8; Thomas, Gwynn & Adams, Melinda. op. cit., pp. 107, 121. Hence the claim made by Jalazai and Krook that "popular election appears to be limited to women from political families" does not hold for Ellen Johnson-Sirleaf. Jalalzai, Farida & Krook, Mona Lena. op. cit., p. 13.

[30] Adams, Melinda. op. cit., pp. 477, 480; Harris, David. op. cit., pp. 376-377; Thomas, Gwynn & Adams, Melinda. op. cit., pp. 111, 113, 117.

Overall, there is a variety of structural, cultural and institutional factors impeding women's access to decision-making positions power, many of which can be observed in Liberia.[31] Nevertheless, it is noteworthy that

> "women have tended to become presidents and prime ministers in contexts where women's status lags far behind that of men in the educational and economic spheres, and in places where women face numerous constraints on their political and social participation".[32]

This implies that despite adverse conditions, there are factors favouring the success of individual women, which will be discussed in the following. To begin with, women's increasing political participation is taken up, before specificities of post-conflict settings are assessed. Finally, the relevance of gender needs consideration.

There is a tendency to focus on Ellen Johnson-Sirleaf as the first female elected president in Africa. This perspective conceals that she is far from being the first woman in a leadership position. Throughout the African continent, female politicians increasingly run for or hold executive positions and are members of parliament.[33] Johnson-Sirleaf herself was preceded by her compatriot Ruth Perry who chaired the Council of State of the transitional government (1996-1997). This tendency should not be overestimated as women in leadership positions remain underrepresented and it is questionable what influence they effectively wield. Nevertheless, her victory must be seen against a background where women increasingly access power positions and gain approval.[34]

It is often argued that post-conflict contexts are particularly hostile to women. Conflicts and post-conflict settings clearly have harmful consequences such

---

[31] See chapter 3.2. and 6.2.

[32] Jalalzai and Krook point out that there seems to be a correlation between lower levels of parity between the two genders and women in power. Jalalzai, Farida & Krook, Mona Lena. op. cit., p. 7.

[33] Adams, Melinda. op. cit., pp. 476-478; Inter-Parliamentary Union (IPU). *Women in National Parliaments* [Website]. 2011. Available online at: http://www.ipu.org/wmn-e/world.htm (Accessed on 04 May 2012); Jalalzai, Farida & Krook, Mona Lena. op. cit., pp. 6-10, 15-17.

[34] According to Afrobarometer statistics, 74 per cent "of Africans [...] agreed with the notion that women should have the same chance of being elected to political office as men". Adams, Melinda. op. cit., p. 477.

as increased levels of domestic and gender based violence, the militarisation of society, which negatively modifies masculinities, etc.[35] However, in some instances armed conflict can also help to overcome patriarchal social structures and empower women as they adopt new responsibilities during the conflict and gain experience and skills, which they use to impact post-conflict developments.[36] According to Adams, this together with the fact that new institutions are created after conflicts and the political space opens up explains why women's representation often increases in post-conflict situations.[37] Jalalzai and Krook adopt a slightly different perspective by stressing that contexts of political instability and weak institutions favour women's access to leadership positions.[38] Differentiated examination is required as to in how far post-conflict settings empower women, leave their often difficult living conditions unchanged, or even deteriorate them. Effects of modifications in gender relations vary across societal domains and affect different individual and groups of women – and men – in different ways.[39] Hence, the fact that gender discrimination remained pronounced in Liberia after the civil war does not contradict Ellen Johnson-Sirleaf's success. On the contrary, being highly educated and a member of the political elite, she benefitted from very specific opportunities in the aftermath of the conflict.

---

[35] Jones-Demen, Annie. op. cit., p. 111 ; Thomas, Gwynn & Adams, Melinda. op. cit., p. 113.

[36] Adams, Melinda. op. cit., p. 479; Aisha, Fatoumata. 'Mainstreaming Gender in Peace Support Operations: The United Nations Mission in Liberia'. In: Aboagye, Festus & Bah, Alahji (eds.). *A Tortuous Road to Peace: The Dynamics of Regional, UN and International Humanitarian Interventions in Liberia*. Pretoria, Publications of the Institute of Security Studies, 2005, p. 150. For a more detailed and differentiated analysis of the impacts of the Liberian conflict on women's lives, see section 4.1.

[37] Adams, Melinda. op. cit., p. 479. Women's representation increased, for instance, after conflicts in Rwanda (56.3 per cent), the country with the highest percentage of women in parliament in the world, and Mozambique (39.2 per cent). However, a high percentage of women in parliament is not necessarily an indicator for greater gender equality in society or attention paid to gender issues. Burnet, Jennie E. 'Gender Balance and the Meaning of Women in Governance in Post-Genocide Rwanda'. In: *African Affairs*, Vol. 107, No. 428, 2008, pp. 378-381; IPU. op. cit.

[38] Jalalzai, Farida & Krook, Mona Lena. op. cit., pp. 8, 13.

[39] In Liberia, despite some improvements regarding gender equality and equity in the post-conflict context, positive tendencies are outweighed by negative ones, as the examination of different societally relevant domains underlines. See chapter 6.1.

Another aspect connected to the post-conflict context that contributed to Johnson-Sirleaf's electoral success was the emergence of the women's movement during the conflict. Its impact requires nuanced consideration and must not be overestimated, as it is far from clear that women's engagement leads to their greater representation or participation in politics.[40] In Liberia, for example, the women's movement did not succeed in introducing a quota and few, mainly urban women obtained seats in parliament.[41] Nevertheless, the activity of the movement indirectly helped Johnson-Sirleaf. It had created a political climate where women's participation had obtained legitimacy, which served as an ideational foundation for her campaign.[42] In more concrete terms, by rising awareness, women's organisationss also helped to increase the number of female registered voters from 30 to almost 50 per cent. It is broadly assumed that Johnson-Sirleaf won thanks to the votes of women of different ethnic origin and social status as well as the support of the Americo-Liberian elite.[43]

Thomas and Adams argue that

"[o]nce women enter races, gender stereotypes influence how the public and the media perceive candidates and how individual candidates present them-selves".[44]

Hence, the role of cultural perceptions of gender and their use in election campaigns deserve attention. Ellen Johnson-Sirleaf who is called Liberia's "Iron Lady" and "Ma Ellen" effectively used a double strategy in order to ex-ploit gendered notions regarding men and women. By doing so, she aimed at benefitting from gendered advantages, while countering potential disad-vantages related to gender.[45] On the one hand, Johnson-Sirleaf stressed her

---

[40] Chapter 6.2. will more closely analyse why women's movements did not lead to greater female participation after the conflict.

[41] Integrated Regional Information Networks (IRIN). *Analysis: Do Liberians Know What They're Voting for?* [Website]. 05 August, 2011. Available online at: http://www.irin news.org/Report/93431/Analysis-Do-Liberians-know-what-they-re-voting-for (Accessed on 10 May 2012); IPU. op. cit. See also chapter 6.1.

[42] Thomas, Gwynn & Adams, Melinda. op. cit., pp. 114-115, 117, 127.

[43] Adams, Melinda. op. cit., pp. 477, 482; Harris, David. op. cit., p. 381, 390; Jalalzai, Fa-rida & Krook, Mona Lena. op. cit., p. 8; Thomas, Gwynn & Adams, Melinda. op. cit., p. 122, 127.

[44] Thomas, Gwynn & Adams, Melinda. op. cit., p. 111. See also ibid., p. 117.

[45] Ibid., pp. 106, 124, 127-128.

'masculine' leadership qualities, for example her experiences as an economist and politician. These were meant to demonstrate that she was capable of satisfying the requirements of a field which is often perceived as an area of male expertise.[46] On the other hand, she highlighted the advantages of a female president, such as women's alleged ability to promote peace, to reconcile or to fight corruption, which resonated with the post-conflict context.[47] Thus, not only did she "challenge connections between masculinity and political leadership by first portraying [herself] as capable [leader] in terms of traditional characteristics"[48] but she also questioned "the connection between masculinity and political leadership by highlighting the particular benefits [she] possessed as [a woman]".[49] It is certainly more than disputable if these essentialist attributions actually reflect reality, but they seem to be helpful in a post-conflict context where these very qualities are needed and where there is a certain frustration regarding male leadership.[50] Overall, gender identity and gender ideology clearly played a role in Ellen Johnson-Sirleaf's electoral success, as they were skilfully used to highlight that she was as suited for the position as any man – and potentially even better – in the particular situation.

In the case of Liberia, there were certainly socio-economic, cultural and institutional obstacles impeding women's access to power. However, other structural and individual factors such as the specific post-conflict context or the strategic combination of gendered stereotypes with personal experience considerably favoured Ellen Johnson-Sirleaf. Therefore, her electoral victory is not as surprising as it seems at first sight. The interaction of a variety of different and sometimes contradicting influences also demonstrates that their

---

[46] Cantrell, Tania H. & Bachmann, Ingrid. op. cit., pp. 430-431; Thomas, Gwynn & Adams, Melinda. op. cit., pp. 118, 121, 124. This discourse was sometimes harshly criticised, as she allegedly gave up her womanhood and turned herself into a "category-less, sexless being" in order to succeed in a male-dominated society and domain. Wrong, Michela. 'World View - Michela Wrong Doubts If a Woman Is Any Better'. In: New Statesman, 28 November, 2005. Available online at: http://www.newstatesman.com/node/152092 (Accessed on 09 May 2012).

[47] Adams, Melinda. op. cit., pp. 482-483; Cantrell, Tania H. & Bachmann, Ingrid. op. cit., pp. 436, 439; Jalalzai, Farida & Krook, Mona Lena. op. cit., p. 11; Thomas, Gwynn & Adams, Melinda. op. cit., pp. 106, 117, 122, 125-126.

[48] Thomas, Gwynn & Adams, Melinda. op. cit., p. 124.

[49] Ibid., p. 124.

[50] Adams, Melinda. op. cit., p. 483; Thomas, Gwynn & Adams, Melinda. op. cit., p. 121

differentiated examination is imperative. The example of Johnson-Sirleaf further underlines that an individual woman's success is possible despite a generally gender-insensitive background. Thus, neither does the degree of gender sensitivity of a society indicate in how far women can succeed in gaining leadership positions, nor does the effective success of female individuals tell anything about the general situation of women in society.[51]

5.3. Between continuity and a political new start: The first Johnson-Sirleaf administration

When Ellen Johnson-Sirleaf was inaugurated in 2006, she assumed the leadership of a country devastated by 14 years of civil strife and several decades of bad governance and economic mismanagement. In her inaugural address she identified "Security, Economic Revitalization, Basic Services, Infrastructure, and Good Governance"[52] as the major challenges. This indicates that Liberia could hardly be restored, but had to be reinvented.[53] As Johnson-Sirleaf has accomplished her first term in office, the question is to what extent she succeeded in addressing these issues? While she is celebrated in Western countries where she is depicted as the "best president the country has ever had",[54] she faces strong criticism in her own country.[55] Hence, this section will critically assess some of the major achievements and failures of the first administration of Johnson-Sirleaf regarding security, fighting corruption, reconciliation and economic development. It is too early and beyond the scope of this chapter to fully evaluate the work of her administration.[56] Hence, the overall aim is not to judge the performance of the government and decide

---

[51] Jalalzai, Farida & Krook, Mona Lena. op. cit., p. 7.
[52] Johnson-Sirleaf, Ellen. *Inaugural Address (16 January 2006)*. 2006, p. 6. Available online at: http://www.emansion.gov.lr/doc/inaugural_add_1.pdf (Accessed on 25 July 2011). See also Ackerman, Ruthie. 'Rebuilding Liberia, One Brick at a Time'. In: *World Policy Journal*, Vol. 26, No. 2, 2009, p. 84.
[53] Stephen Ellis as quoted in Benner, Thorsten & Blume, Till. op. cit., p. 41.
[54] Economist. *Liberia's Feisty President: Another Round for Africa's Iron Lady: A Woman's Work Is Never Done* [Website]. 20 May, 2010. Available online at: http://www.economist.com/node/16168384 (Accessed on 04 May 2012).
[55] Cantrell, Tania H. & Bachmann, Ingrid. op. cit., pp. 442.
[56] For an in-depth evaluation of Liberia's post-conflict development, see ICG. op. cit., *Liberia. How Sustainable is the Recovery?*.

whether support or criticism of Johnson-Sirleaf's work during her first term of office is justified, but to identify and understand difficulties that continue to plague the country.

The security situation in Liberia has considerably improved. However, stability is largely provided by external forces, namely the UNMIL, whose mandate was prolonged several times.[57] Despite deficiencies and delays in the beginning, the security sector reform (SSR) has made progress and can be considered largely successful.[58] Nevertheless, a variety of difficulties remain within the security forces, for example misbehaviour, corruption and human rights abuses as well as a lack of equipment and personnel. These challenges cause doubts regarding the quality of security forces and in particular, their capacity to effectively provide security throughout the Liberian territory.[59] At the same time security challenges persist inside the country due to ex-combatants and criminality, social tensions and protest, but also as poverty and a lack of perspectives prevail. Furthermore, Liberia's stability is adversely affected by the political situation in the sub-region and neighbouring Guinea and Côte d'Ivoire in particular. Security menaces consist among other things in the influx of arms and refugees and activities of ex-combatants in bordering regions.[60]

Another key challenge of the Liberian government is fighting corruption. In 2005, the National Transitional Government of Liberia and external donors

[57] Ackerman, Ruthie. op. cit., p. 83; ICG. op. cit., *Liberia: How Sustainable is the Recovery?*, pp. 11, 26. Cook, Nikolas. *CRS Report for Congress: Liberia's Post-War Recovery: Key Issues and Developments.* Washington D.C., Congressional Research Service, 2007, p. 13; Available online at: http://www.fas.org/sgp/crs/row/RL33185.pdf (Accessed on 25 July 2011; United Nations Security Council (UNSC). *Resolution 2008 (2011).* New York, 2011. Available online at: http://www.un.org/ga/search/view_doc.asp?symbol=S/RES/2008%282011%29 (Accessed on 25 May 2012). The UNMIL is currently authorised until 30 September 2012.

[58] Jaye, Thomas. *Transitional Justice and DDR: The Case of Liberia.* New York, International Center for Transitional Justice, 2009, p. 17. Available online at: http://ictj.org/sites/default/files/ICTJ-DDR-Liberia-CaseStudy-2009-English.pdf (Accessed on 25 May 2012); Nilsson, Desirée & Söderberg Kovacs, Mimmi. op cit., pp. 404, 411.

[59] ICG. op. cit., *Liberia. How Sustainable is the Recovery?*, pp. 11-13.

[60] Ackerman, Ruthie. op. cit., p. 89; Cook, Nikolas. op. cit., pp. 14-15; ICG. op. cit., *Liberia: How Sustainable is the Recovery?*, pp. 11, 14; Nilsson, Desirée & Söderberg Kovacs, Mimmi. op cit., pp. 400, 409-410 .

signed the Governance and Economic Management Assistance Programme in order to confront "serious corruption and mismanagement of public finances in post-conflict Liberia" and improve "public finance management and accountability".[61] It provided for international oversight regarding economic and fiscal transactions, which is why it was partly criticised for challenging the country's sovereignty, and foresaw further legal steps, such as the creation of an Anti-Corruption Commission.[62] The Johnson-Sirleaf administration established the latter in 2008 and took further legal steps to reduce corruption.[63] However, in 2011 Liberia ranked 91 out of 183 in the Transparency International Corruption Perceptions Index and obtained a score of 3.2 out of 10.[64] This indicates that despite some success, corruption remains endemic and an integral part of Liberian authority, including the government.[65] Legal acts and institutions resemble paper tigers or watchdogs without teeth as they lack power and their activities often do not generate repercussions, such as prosecution or conviction of perpetrators. Overall, there seems to be a lack political will and commitment to effectively tackle corruption.[66] Fighting corruption certainly takes a long time. However, according to William Reno, the problem "is not just the extent of Liberia's corruption, but that the *organization of corruption* in Liberia reflects social relations".[67] Hence, while corruption continues

---

[61] Dwan, Renata & Bailey, Laura. *Liberia's Governance and Economic Management Assistance Programme (GEMAP): A joint review by the Department of Peacekeeping Operations' Peacekeeping Best Practices Section and the World Bank's Fragile States Group.* New York/Washington D.C., UN Department of Peacekeeping Operations/The World Bank, 2006, p. 6. Available online at: http://www.pbpu.unlb.org/PBPS/Library/DPKO-WB%20joint%20review%20of%20GEMAP%20FINAL.pdf (Accessed on 24 May 2012).

[62] Ibid., p. 6; Nilsson, Desirée & Söderberg-Kovacs, Mimmi. op cit., p. 408; Reno, Williams. 'Anti-corruption Efforts in Liberia: Are They Aimed at the Right Targets?' In: *International Peacekeeping*, Vol. 15, No. 3, 2008, p. 387.

[63] ICG. op. cit., *Liberia: How Sustainable is the Recovery?*, p. 18. A detailed overview of the different measures is provided by Cook, Nicolas. op. cit., pp. 28-34.

[64] Transparency International. *Corruption by Country/Territory* [Website]. 2011. Available online at: http://www.transparency.org/country#LBR_DataResearch_SurveysIndices (Accessed on 24 May 2012). While a score of zero indicates that a country is highly corrupt, a score of ten is the best result possible.

[65] ICG. op. cit., *Liberia. How Sustainable is the Recovery?*, pp. 17-18; Reno, Williams. op. cit., pp. 387-388, 398.

[66] ICG. op. cit., *Liberia: How Sustainable is the Recovery?*, p. 18; IRIN. op. cit., *Analysis*.

[67] Reno, Williams. op. cit., p. 400; emphasis in the original.

to represent a threat to stability, the current means to address corruption might be revealed ineffectual.[68]

Questions of security and corruption are connected to the performance and quality of the justice sector, which is supposed to guarantee the rule of law, hold perpetrators of crime responsible and fight the prevailing culture of impunity.[69] However, the Liberian judicial system is weak and overstretched; so far, reforms were only slowly undertaken leaving the judiciary ill-prepared and incapable – or unwilling – to contribute its share.[70]

The Comprehensive Peace Agreement signed in 2003 foresaw a Truth and Reconciliation Commission to "deal with the root causes of the crises in Liberia, including human rights violations" and "to facilitate genuine healing and reconciliation".[71] However, the work of the TRC is controversial both within and outside Liberia.[72] On the one hand, by recording more than 20,000 statements in Liberia and abroad, it gathered encompassing, in-depth information about economic and various other crimes and human rights violations during the conflict and afforded victims an opportunity to speak about their

---

[68] Corruption is seen as one of the major causes of conflict in Liberia. ICG. op. cit., *Liberia: How Sustainable is the Recovery?*, p. 17. See also Nilsson, Desirée & Söderberg Kovacs, Mimmi. op. cit., p. 406.

[69] Ackerman, Ruthie. op. cit., p. 88 ; ICG. op. cit., *Liberia: How Sustainable is the Recovery?*, p. 14; Nilsson, Desirée & Söderberg Kovacs, Mimmi. op. cit., pp. 404-405.

[70] Ackerman, Ruthie. op. cit., p. 88; ICG. op. cit., *Liberia: How Sustainable is the Recovery?*, p. 18; Reno, Williams. op. cit., p. 398 See also chapter 6.1.

[71] *Comprehensive Peace Agreement between the Government of Liberia and the Liberians United for Reconciliation and Democracy (LURD) and the Movement for Democracy in Liberia (MODEL) and Political Parties.* 2003, art. XIII, 2 and 1. Available online at: http://www.usip.org/files/file/resources/collections/peace_agreements/liberia_08182003 .pdf (Accessed on 23 July 2011). See also Hayner, Priscilla B. *Unspeakable Truths: Transitional Justice and the Challenge of Truth Commissions.* Abingdon, Routledge, 2011, p. 66.

[72] Hayner, Priscilla B. op. cit., 67-68; ICG. op. cit., *Liberia: How Sustainable is the Recovery?*, p. 19; Integrated Regional Information Networks (IRIN). *Liberia: Opinion Divided on Truth and Reconciliation Findings* [Website]. 06 July, 2011. Available online at: http://www.irinnews.org/Report/85158/LIBERIA-Opinion-divided-on-Truth-and-Reconciliation-findings (Accessed on 10 May 2012); Jaye, Thomas. op. cit., *Transitional Justice and DDR*, p. 21. A detailed discussion of the contributions and shortfalls of the TRC in Liberia is beyond the scope of this chapter, but is available in Paul, James-Allen; Weah, Aaron & Goodfriend, Lizzy. *Beyond the Truth and Reconciliation Commission: Transitional Justice Options in Liberia.* New York, International Center for Transitional Justice, 2010, pp. 13-17. Available online at: https://ictj.org/sites/default/files/ ICTJ-Liberia-Beyond-TRC-2010-English.pdf (Accessed on 27 May 2012).

experiences.[73] It made recommendations on a variety of issues that need attention in order to promote reconciliation such as an amnesty for children implicated in the fighting, the instauration of community-based mechanisms of conflict resolution, reparations and criminal responsibility for perpetrators of war crimes.[74] On the other hand, the Commission was criticised, among others, for inconsistency in its findings, procedural difficulties and for serving as a platform for perpetrators without inducing prosecution.[75] The 2009 report published by the TRC especially caused contention: Its most famous proposition was probably to ban Ellen Johnson-Sirleaf from office together with 48 other – seemingly arbitrarily compiled – individuals due to "their roles during the years of war and instability in Liberia".[76] This raised questions about the politicisation of the TRC and pushed the other recommendations into the rear.[77] Deliberations about reconciliation must look beyond the work of the Truth and Reconciliation Commission and include other actors and domains. Although disputed as well, a remarkable step taken by Johnson-Sirleaf was to promote Charles Taylor's extradition, who had sought exile in Nigeria. As a consequence, he did not remain unpunished, but was judged by the Special Court for Sierra Leone.[78] However, critics point out that this does not counterbalance prevailing impunity and that apart from this the government took little action, which is why the findings of the Truth and Reconciliation Commission

---

[73] Hayner, Priscilla B. op. cit., 67; Jaye, Thomas. op. cit., *Transitional Justice and DDR*; p. 20; Jaye, Thomas. *Research Brief: Transitional Justice and DDR: The Case of Liberia.* New York, International Center for Transitional Justice, 2009, p. 3. Available online at: http://ictj.org/sites/default/files/ICTJ-DDR-Liberia-ResearchBrief-2009-English_0.pdf (Accessed on 25 May 2012).

[74] Paul, James-Allen; Weah, Aaron & Goodfriend, Lizzy. op. cit., pp. 13-14.

[75] Hayner, Priscilla B. op. cit., p. 67; ICG. op. cit., *Liberia : How Sustainable is the Recovery?*, p. 20; Integrated Regional Information Networks (IRIN). *Liberia: TRC Furore Overshadows Peace Building Proposals* [Website]. 09 July, 2009. Available online at: http://www.irinnews.org/Report/85215/LIBERIA-TRC-furore-overshadows-peace-buil ding-proposals (Accessed on 10 May 2012); Jaye, Thomas. op. cit., pp. 22-23; Paul, James-Allen; Weah, Aaron & Goodfriend, Lizzy. op. cit., pp. 14, 16. Available online at: https://ictj.org/sites/default/files/ICTJ-Liberia-Beyond-TRC-2010-English.pdf (Accessed on 27 May 2012).

[76] TRC. op. cit., p. 361.

[77] Hayner, Priscilla B. op. cit., p. 68; ICG. op. cit., *Liberia: How Sustainable is the Recovery?*, p. 19; IRIN. op. cit., *Liberia: Opinion Divided*; Paul, James-Allen; Weah, Aaron & Goodfriend, Lizzy. op. cit., p. 16.

[78] There, he was indicted for his implication in the conflict in Sierra Leone. In Liberia itself, no cases of war crimes were taken up. Jaye, Thomas. op. cit., *Transitional Justice and DDR*, p. 23.

were only slowly or not at all implemented.[79] Given that reconciliation is an active process that requires commitment, it is questionable in how far reconciliation can or will become a reality in Liberia.

In economic terms, the Johnson-Sirleaf administration has made some very visible progress. In 2010, the country benefitted from a debt relief of $4.6 billion within the framework of the Heavily Indebted Poor Countries Initiative.[80] International bans on timber and diamonds, which were launched during the conflict, were lifted.[81] In addition, foreign direct investment was attracted particularly in the extractive and the agricultural sector. On the shady sight, external investments often provoke tensions between foreign companies and local communities over land rights and do not necessarily create jobs for Liberians.[82] Entrepreneurship on a small or medium scale is hindered by structural obstacles such as a lack of infrastructure or difficulties regarding loans and taxpaying. Overall, the informal economy makes up a disproportional share of economic activity providing four-fifths of the workforce and poverty remains high.[83]

In spite of important improvements, various problems persist. Hence, the doubtlessly high expectations regarding Johnson-Sirleaf's presidency were belied to some extent. However, reconstruction and development require time, resources and capacity, all of which have been scarce in Liberia. In addition, policy making is complicated by deeply rooted and often conflicting interests, including those of formerly warring parties, and the functioning of political institutions. While compromise is required, far reaching changes are difficult to achieve.[84] This underlines that purely personal criticism is inadequate and misleading, as it fails to consider structural obstacles. It also distracts at-

---

[79] Ackerman, Ruthie. op. cit., p. 86-87; ICG. op. cit., *Liberia: How Sustainable is the Recovery?*, p. 20; IRIN. op. cit., *Analysis;* Jaye, Thomas. op. cit., *Transitional Justice and DDR* , p. 23; Nilsson, Desirée & Söderberg Kovacs, Mimmi. op cit., p. 407.
[80] ICG. op. cit., *Liberia. How Sustainable is the Recovery?*, p. 21.
[81] Cook, Nikolas. op. cit., pp. 9-10, 14.
[82] ICG. op. cit., *Liberia: How Sustainable is the Recovery?*, pp. 21-22; IRIN. op. cit., *Analysis.* Among the contractors that are regularly mentioned are China Union, Arcelor Mittal and Chevron.
[83] ICG. op. cit., *Liberia: How Sustainable is the Recovery?*, p. 22.
[84] Thomas, Gwynn & Adams, Melinda. Op. cit., p. 127.

tention from the actual problems impeding the country to effectively advance and recover from its past, which require concerted and comprehensive efforts.

After having contextualised and examined Ellen Johnson-Sirleaf's election and the controversies surrounding her personality and work, it is now necessary to explicitly assess developments in post-conflict Liberia through a gender lens and examine them against the background of masculinity in order to draw theoretical conclusions.

6. Peace at last? A critical analysis of Liberia's Post-Conflict situation

Women were strongly involved in peacemaking and peacebuilding in Liberia and various recent official documents refer to gender issues.[1] In addition, a female president accessed power in 2005 and promised to pay particular attention to women's issues and empowerment.[2] Therefore, it could be assumed that the situation of Liberian women has improved. However, the country's ranking in gender indices shows that this is not the case.[3] Hence, while the previous chapter focused on developments in post-conflict Liberia in general terms, the final chapter evaluates modern day Liberia in terms of gender sensitivity; it discusses factors impeding its emergence, the influence of masculinity is especially looked at, and draws theoretical conclusions.

6.1. Deficient peace? A multi-factorial analysis of the Liberian post-conflict order through a gender lens

In chapter 2.1., a multi-dimensional notion of peace was developed. Based on this, the Liberian post-conflict order will now be evaluated and political, security, legal and socio-economic as well as socio-cultural challenges and achievements will be identified. Here, the individual (micro), community or sub-state (mezzo) and state (macro) levels are observed and external influ-

---

[1]   See, for example, *Comprehensive Peace Agreement between the Government of Liberia and the Liberians United for Reconciliation and Democracy (LURD) and the Movement for Democracy in Liberia (MODEL) and Political Parties*. 2003. Available online at: http://www.usip.org/files/file/resources/collections/peace_agreements/liberia_08182003 .pdf (Accessed on 23 July 2011); Government of Liberia. *150 Day Action Plan: A Working Document for a New Liberia*. Undated. Available online at: http://allafrica.com/ peaceafrica/resources/view/00010785.pdf (Accessed on 25 July 2011); Johnson-Sirleaf, Ellen. *Inaugural Address (16 January 2006)*. 2006. Available online at: http:// www.emansion.gov.lr/doc/inaugural_add_1.pdf (Accessed on 25 July 2011).

[2]   Johnson-Sirleaf, Ellen. op. cit., *Inaugural Address*, p. 12.

[3]   Organisation for Economic Co-operation and Development Social Institutions and Gender Index (OECD-SIGI). *Gender Equality and Social Institutions in Liberia* [Website]. 2011. Available online at: http://www.genderindex.org/country/Liberia (Accessed on 21 July 2011); United Nations Development Programme (UNDP). *Liberia: Country Profile of Human Development Indicators* [Website]. New York, 2011. Available online at: http://hdrstats.undp.org/en/*countries*/profiles/LBR.html (Accessed on 18 June 2011).

ences included.[4] Afterwards, conclusions about structural obstacles are drawn.

a) Political challenges

In the 2005 national elections, women represented approximately half of the registered voters. The number of women's civil society organisations in various areas such as agriculture and politics or self-help groups shows that female activism remained stable after the conflict.[5] A qualitative assessment of their influence is beyond the scope of this thesis. This is why their influence can only be assumed, as they are often externally funded, but not measured.[6] Today, the executive is not only led by a female president, but female politicians account for 30 per cent of the cabinet and hold high offices and positions. In 2001, a Gender and Development ministry was created and there are attempts to integrate women in all policies.[7] However, in the legislature elected in 2005, women held only 12.5 per cent of the seats in the House of Representatives and 16.7 per cent in the Senate. After the 2011 parliamentary elections, the average of female members even dropped to 9.6 and 13.3 per

---

[4] A detailed overview of the results of the analysis can be found in Appendix III.
[5] Fuest, Veronika. "This is the Time to Get in Front': Changing Roles and Opportunities for Women in Liberia'. In: *African Affairs*, Vol. 107, No. 427, 2008, p. 213; Governance Commission of Liberia. *Beyond Numbers: An Assessment of the Liberian Civil Society: A Report on the CIVICUS Civil Society Index 2010*. 2011. Available online at: http://www.civicus.org/images/stories/csi/csi_phase2/Liberia_ACR_final.pdf (Accessed on 26 July 2011). See also African Women and Peace Support Group. *Liberian Women Peacemakers: Fighting for the Right to Be Seen, Heard, and Counted*. Trenton, Africa World Press, 2004.
[6] Fuest, Veronika. op. cit., p. 213.
[7] African Women and Peace Support Group. op. cit., p. 56; Central Intelligence Agency (CIA). *Liberia: Chiefs of State and Cabinet Members of Foreign Governments* [Website]. 2011. Available online at: https://www.cia.gov/library/publications/world-leaders-1/world-leaders-I/liberia.html (Accessed on 25 July 2011); Fuest, Veronika. op. cit., pp. 215-216; Kellow, Tim. *Women, Elections and Violence in West Africa: Assessing Women's Political Participation in Liberia and Sierra Leone*. London, International Alert, 2010, p. 18. Available online at: http://www.international-alert.org/sites/default/files/publications/201012WomenElectionsViolenceWestAfrica.pdf (Accessed on 20 July 2011); OECD-SIGI. op. cit.; Svensson, Katja. 'Women Hold up Half the Sky: Peace and Security Lessons from Liberia'. In: *African Security Review*, Vol. 17, No. 4, 2008, p. 179; United Nations General Assembly. *Liberia Is Writing New History for Its Women and Girls Delegation Tells Women's Anti-Discrimination Committee, Admitting Great Challenges in That Endeavour* [Website]. New York, 2009. Available online at: http://www.un.org/News/Press/docs/2009/wom1748.doc.htm (Accessed on 20 July 2011).

cent in the House of Representatives and the Senate, respectively.[8] Hence, although there was an improvement compared to the interwar period, the informally agreed female quota of 30 per cent was not met. Furthermore, former warlords responsible for human rights abuses are members of parliament, which represents a certain negligence of women and their interests.[9]

b) Security challenges

The Liberian security sector reform partly managed to increase women's participation in the security forces, although their share remained lower than intended. Instead of 20 per cent, the army contains only approximately five per cent. Twelve per cent of the police forces are women.[10] Women and children protection units and community policing were introduced and training includes issues on gender, rule of law and human rights. However, international observers especially criticise the reform of the police and argue that the state does not possess a monopoly on violence and the capacity to maintain security, which is why the security situation remains fragile and dependent on private and external actors.[11]

---

[8] In comparison, in 1999, women held two per cent of ministerial as well as one per cent of other executive positions, and made up five per cent in parliament. At the same time, these figures are well beyond the Sub-Saharan average that amounts to 20.4 per cent in the Lower House and 19.4 per cent in the Upper House. African Women and Peace Support Group. op. cit., p. 55; Governance Commission of Liberia. op. cit.; Inter-Parliamentary Union. *Women in National Parliaments* [Website]. 2011. Available online at: http://www.ipu.org/wmn-e/world.htm (Accessed on 04 May 2012); Kellow, Tim. op. cit., pp. 5, 22; Sawyer, Amos. 'Emerging Patterns in Liberia's Post-Conflict Politics: Observations from the 2005 Elections'. In: *African Affairs*, Vol. 107, No. 427, 2008, pp. 187-188; United Nations General Assembly. op. cit., *Liberia Is Writing New History*.

[9] Cook, Nikolas. CRS Report for Congress: *Liberia's Post-War Recovery: Key Issues and Developments*. Washington D.C., Congressional Research Service, 2007, pp. 7-8. Available online at: http://www.fas.org/sgp/crs/row/RL33185.pdf (Accessed on 25 July 2011); Mehler, Andreas & Smith-Höhn, Judy. 'Liberia: Ellen in Wonderland?' In: *GIGA Fokus*, No. 5, 2006, pp. 4, 7. Available online at: http://www.giga-hamburg.de/dl/download.php?d=/content/publikationen/pdf/gf_afrika_0605.pdf (Accessed on 20 July 2011).

[10] Fuest, Veronika. op. cit., p. 216, ICG. op. cit., *Liberia: Uneven Progress*, pp. 11-12, 18. A detailed discussion of the SSR can be found in International Crisis Group (ICG). *Liberia: Uneven Progress in Security Sector Reform*. Africa Report No. 148, 2009, pp. 4-5. Available online at: http://www.crisisgroup.org/en/regions/africa/west-africa/liberia/148-liberia-uneven-progress-in-security-sector-reform.aspx (Accessed on 20 July 2011).

[11] ICG. op. cit., *Liberia: Uneven Progress*, pp. 1, 5-8, 14, 17, 19, 22, 30; Krasno, Jean. *External Study: Public Opinion Survey of UNMIL's Work in Liberia*. New York, 2006, pp. 5, 16. Available online at: http://pbpu.unlb.org/PBPS/Library/Liberia_POS_final_report

The DDRR programme included women and girls.[12] But there were many qualitative deficiencies. Women's groups were not included in the planning and implementation of the DDRR despite their commitment and experience.[13] Neither were there the necessary female personnel, e.g. military observers, nor knowledge about women's specific needs.[14] Furthermore, women lacked adequate information about the process. Often, they did not participate at all, dropped out prematurely or benefitted only partly from the measures due to insufficient funding.[15] Even if women accomplished the entire DDRR, the support provided did not necessarily enable them to gain their livings after-wards, leaving them in precarious and unsecure living conditions.[16]

_Mar_29.pdfhtml (Accessed on 28 July 2011); Mehler, Andreas & Smith-Höhn, Judy. op. cit., p. 4; Reisinger, Christian. 'A Framework for the Analysis of Post-conflict Situations: Liberia and Mozambique Reconsidered. In: *International Peacekeeping*, Vol. 16, No. 4, 2009, pp. 492-493; United Nations General Assembly. op. cit., *Liberia Is Writing New History*. See also chapter 5.3.

[12] Of the participants, 21 per cent (20,319) were women and two percent girls (2,414) girls. Aboagye, Festus B., Bah & Alhaji M. S. *Liberia at a Crossroads: A Preliminary Look at the United Nations Mission in Liberia (UNMIL) and the Protection of Civilians*. Pretoria, Institute of Security Studies (Occasional Paper No. 95), 2004. Available online at: http://www.iss.org.za/pubs/papers/95/Paper95.htm (Accessed on 28 June 2011).

[13] African Women and Peace Support Group. op. cit.; Conciliation Resources. *Accord Liberia Project* [Website]. 2011. Available online at: http://www.c-r.org/our-work/accord/liberia/index.php (Accessed on 08 July 2011); Amnesty International (AI). *Lessons from Liberia: Reintegrating Women in Postconflict Liberia*. 2009. Available online at: http://www.amnesty.org/en/library/asset/AFR34/002/2009/en/442e0181-c8e2-4057-81f6-d19 ceddf0045/afr340022009en.pdf (Accessed on 28 June 2011); Disney, Abigail E. & Reticker, Gini (dirs.). *Pray the Devil Back to Hell* [DVD Documentary]. New York, Fork Films, 2008.

[14] Aisha, Fatoumata. 'Mainstreaming Gender in Peace Support Operations: The United Nations Mission in Liberia'. In: Aboagye, Festus & Bah, Alahji (eds.). *A Tortuous Road to Peace: The Dynamics of Regional, UN and International Humanitarian Interventions in Liberia*. Pretoria, Publications of the Institute of Security Studies, 2005, p. 157.

[15] Amnesty International (AI). *Liberia: A Flawed Process Discriminates against Women and Girls*. 2008, pp. 21, 34, 36-36. Available online at: http://www.amnesty.org/en/library/asset/AFR34/004/2008/en/c075d220-00cf-11dd-a9d5-b31ac3ea5bcc/afr3400 42008eng.pdf (Accessed on 04 July 2011); AI. op. cit., *Lessons from Liberia*; Thomas, Gwynn & Adams, Melinda. 'Breaking the Final Glass Ceiling: The Influence of Gender in the Elections of Ellen Johnson-Sirleaf and Michelle Bachelet'. In: *Journal of Women*, Vol. 31, No. 2, 2010, p. 108.

[16] Aboagye, Festus B. & Bah, Alhaji M. S. op. cit.; AI. op. cit., *Lessons from Liberia*; Aisha, Fatoumata. op. cit., p. 157; Bennett, Olivia et al. (eds.). *Arms to Fight, Arms to Protect: Women Speak out about Conflict*. London, Panos, 1995, p. 39; ICG. op. cit., *Liberia: Uneven Progress*, p. 27; Thomas, Gwynn & Adams, Melinda. op. cit., p. 108; United Nations General Assembly. op. cit., *Liberia Is Writing New History*.

In addition, the conflict led to an increased level of gender-based violence, which includes among others discrimination on various issues, physical and sexual assaults as well as abuse, and its societal tolerance.[17] Among other factors, this is facilitated by the circulation of SALW, deficient infrastructure and the erosion of moral norms and social constraints during the civil war. Gender crimes often remain unprosecuted or weakly punished, leading to and consolidating a culture of impunity.[18]

c) Legal challenges

In legal terms, the Liberian constitution interdicts discrimination of women, however, there are no specific regulations against gender discrimination.[19] A major difficulty is the legal dualism, i.e. the co-existence of statutory and customary law. Within the former, new laws, e.g. on inheritance or rape, regulate women's rights relating to property, custody and declare rape a criminal offence that is more strictly punished (Rape Amendment Act, 2006).[20] But they are only partially applied, while customary law persists, obstructs their

---

[17] Aisha, Fatoumata. op. cit., p. 147; Ackerman, Ruthie. 'Rebuilding Liberia, One Brick at a Time'. In: *World Policy Journal*, Vol. 26, No. 2, 2009, p. 87.

[18] African Women and Peace Support Group. op. cit., pp. 56-57; Aisha, Fatoumata. op. cit., pp. 158-159; Association of Female Lawyers of Liberia (AFELL) & The Editors. 'Hundreds of Victims Silently Grieving. In: Turshen, Meredeth & Twagiramariya, Clotilde (eds.). *What Women Do in Wartime*. London, Zed Books, 1998, p. 130; ICG. op. cit., *Liberia: Uneven Progress*, pp. 5, 8, 30; OECD-SIGI. op. cit.; Pankhurst, Donna. 'Post-War Backlash Violence against Women: What Can "Masculinity" Explain?' In: ibid. (ed.). *Gendered Peace: Women's Struggles for Post-War Justice and Reconciliation*. London, Routledge, 2008, p. s306; United Nations General Assembly. op. cit., *Liberia Is Writing New History*.

[19] Afrol News. *Gender Profile: Liberia* [Website]. Undated. Available online at: www.afrol.com/Categories/Women/profiles/liberia_women.htm (Accessed on 21 July 2011); Aisha, Fatoumata. op. cit., p. 149; *Constitution of the Republic of Liberia*. 1986, art. 11b. Available online at: http://confinder.richmond.edu/admin/docs/liberia.pdf (Accessed on 21 July 2011); OECD-SIGI. op. cit., United Nations General Assembly. op. cit., *Liberia Is Writing New History*.

[20] Ackerman, Ruthie. op. cit., p. 88; ICG. *Liberia: How Sustainable is the Recovery?* Africa Report No. 177, 2011, p. 13. Available online at: http://www.crisisgroup.org/~/media/Files/africa/west-africa/liberia/177%20Liberia%20-%20How%20Sustainable%20is%20the%20Recovery.pdf (Accessed on 02 May 2012); Jaye, Thomas. *Transitional Justice and DDR: The Case of Liberia*. New York, International Center for Transitional Justice, 2009, p. 24. Available online at: http://ictj.org/sites/default/files/ICTJ-DDR-Liberia-Case Study-2009-English.pdf (Accessed on 25 May 2012).

implementation and discriminates against women and girls.[21] Women also lack access to justice because of their illiteracy, fear or a lack of (financial) means and thus rarely claim their rights. In this context, Ackerman points out that in many cases women do not report sexual crimes to the police, because they fear stigmatisation or that police officers where themselves involved in GBV during the conflict. The International Crisis Group further suggests that they are reluctant to make complaints in order to avoid the imprisonment of members of their community or family. These examples highlight the complex interaction of laws and the societal background they are embedded in.[22] Lastly, there is not enough well-educated legal staff and institutions throughout the country.[23]

It is often highlighted that symbolic progress was made as Ellen Johnson-Sirleaf replaced the inscription of the Supreme Court 'Let justice be done to all men' by the phrase 'Let justice be done to all'.[24] But overall, "the justice sector has made less progress than almost any other",[25] which risks undermining successes in other areas such as the political or security sector.

d) Socio-economic and socio-cultural challenges

Religious, traditional and cultural practices restrict girls' and women's opportunities and determine role patterns and labour division. Despite improve-

---

[21] In customary law, polygamous marriage persists, girls are (forcedly) married at a very early age and women are excluded from access to bank loans, inheriting land, property as well as custody in case of divorce or widowhood. Afrol News. op. cit., *Gender Profile*; Aisha, Fatoumata. op. cit., p.158; Fuest, Veronika. op. cit., pp. 219; ICG. op. cit., *Liberia: Uneven Progress,* pp. 19-20; Mehler, Andreas, Smith-Höhn, Judy. op. cit., p. 6; OECD-SIGI. op. cit.; Richards, Paul. 'Young Men and Gender in War and Postwar Reconstruction: Some Comparative Findings from Liberia and Sierra Leone. In: Bannon, Ian & Correia, Maria C. (eds.). *The Other Half of Gender: Men's Issues in Development.* Washington D.C., The World Bank, 2006, pp. 213-214; Truth and Reconciliation Commission of Liberia. *"Inheritance Law Not Protecting Women"...Attorney Deweh Gray* [Website]. Press Releases, Undated. Available online at: http://trcofliberia. org/press_releases/109 (Accessed on 21July 2011); United Nations General Assembly. op. cit., *Liberia Is Writing New History.*
[22] Ackerman, Ruthie. op. cit., p. 88; ICG. *Liberia: How Sustainable is the Recovery?,* op. cit., p. 13.
[23] Allen, Bonnie. *Liberia: Paper Rights Flimsy Protection* [Website]. Nobel Peace Prize for African Women, 2010. Available online at: http://www.noppaw.net/?p=938pdf (Accessed on 25 July 2011); ICG. op. cit., *Liberia: Uneven Progress,* p. 20.
[24] Ackerman, Ruthie. op. cit., p. 88.
[25] ICG. op. cit., *Liberia: Uneven Progress,* p. 20.

ments in female enrolment and policies to promote girls' education, girls remain underrepresented in school, especially in higher education.[26] They lack qualification, skills and self-confidence, which impacts on their access to material and immaterial resources; for example, women work disproportionally often in the informal and especially the agricultural sector, whereas they are poorly represented in the formal economy. Consequently, women are in many respects economically and socially marginalised and dependent on men, while their opportunities to participate in politics are constrained.[27]

Women also suffer from a deficient health care infrastructure that cannot meet their needs (e.g. treatment of HIV/AIDS, maternal or mental health care).[28] Another problem is female genital mutilation (FGM), which is not prohibited by statutory law. Although having almost disappeared during the war, FGM re-increased after it and considerably affects the physical integrity of women.[29]

e) External influence

Obstacles to a gender-sensitive peace are also found on the sub-regional and international level influencing Liberia during and after the civil war; for example, external actors failed to promote stronger involvement of women in the formal peace process.[30] Both SSR and DDRR were conceptualised as technical, not socio-political projects. Hence, issues of human security and rights

---

[26] Badmus, Alani. 'Explaining Women's Roles in the West African Tragic Triplet: Sierra Leone, Liberia, and Cote d'Ivoire in Comparative Perspective'. In: *Journal of Alternative Perspectives in the Social Sciences*, Vol. 1, No. 3, 2009, p. 834; Bouta, Tsjeard et al. *Gender, Conflict, and Development*. Washington D.C., The World Bank, 2005, p. 71; Fuest, Veronika. op. cit.; United Nations General Assembly. op. cit., *Liberia Is Writing New History*.

[27] Aisha, Fatoumata. op. cit., p. 149, Fuest, Veronika. op. cit., p. 222; Kellow, Tim. op. cit., pp. 6, 19; Richards, Paul. op. cit., p. 214; United Nations General Assembly. op. cit., *Liberia Is Writing New History*.

[28] Aisha, Fatoumata. op. cit., pp. 147, 150; United Nations Development Programme (UNDP). *Liberia Annual Report 2009*. Monrovia, 2009, p. 32. Available online at: http://www.lr.undp.org/Documents/RecentPublic/UNDP%20Liberia%20Annual%20Report%202009.pdf (Accessed on 18 June 2011); United Nations General Assembly. op. cit., *Liberia Is Writing New History*.

[29] Afrol News. op. cit., *Gender Profile*; Aisha, Fatoumata. op. cit., p. 158; OECD-SIGI. op. cit.; United Nations General Assembly. op. cit., *Liberia Is Writing New History*.

[30] This becomes clearly obvious in the analysis of African Women and Peace Support Group. op. cit.

were secondary and gender was inadequately included.[31] Both the Economic Community of West African States and the United Nations lacked female staff and their troops were poorly educated regarding gender issues and even responsible for sexual violence against women.[32] This is hardly a good example for more gender sensitivity or the promotion of women.

In addition, external donors try to promote gender issues by supporting local women's groups. However, their agency in this respect tends to be non-sustainable and exclusive, as especially women's civil society organisations that correspond to Western ideals regarding gender and contribute to the creation of a "'women's solidarity' movement" are backed, while others are neglected.[33] This strategy is unlikely to effectively overcome structural problems. It is also questionable in how far developments actually originate within the society and will be lasting.[34]

This summary shows that, despite achievements, Liberian peace remains gender-insensitive in political, security, legal, socio-economic and socio-cultural terms. Hence, one must ask: why is this the case?

Many of the numerous challenges, e.g. regarding the political system, customary law or socio-cultural norms, are pre-war remains that influenced the Liberian state throughout its existence. They are strongly internalised and thus difficult to overcome. It requires sustained efforts in terms of resources, capacities and especially political will – which are scarce in Liberia – to tackle such structural problems.[35] Constitutional constraints of the political system are another obstacle to reforms. The government promised to undertake and has already taken some steps to promote women.[36] However, the Liberian presidential system is currently in a situation of 'divided government'. As the

---

[31] ICG. op. cit., *Liberia: Uneven Progress*, p. 11.
[32] Aboagye, Festus B. & Bah, Alhaji M. S. op. cit. Aisha, Fatoumata. op. cit., p. 154.
[33] Kellow, Tim. op. cit., p. 16.
[34] Afrol News. *UNMIL Sex Abuse Declines* [Website]. Undated. Available online at: http://www.afrol.com/articles/27647 (Accessed on 28 July 2011); Kellow, Tim. op. cit., p. 16; Krasno, Jean. op. cit., pp. 6, 22.
[35] Kellow, Tim, op. cit., p. 5; United Nations General Assembly. op. cit., *Liberia Is Writing New History*.
[36] Examples are the voting of an 'inheritance law' (2003), a 'rape law' (2005), measures to promote girls' education etc. An overview of the measures is provided by United Nations General Assembly. op. cit., *Liberia Is Writing New History*.

executive does not hold the majority in parliament,[37] its capacity to include gender-mainstreaming, which means that

"all institutional policies and practices are formulated with attention paid to the impact they will have on the individuals as a result of their gender,"[38]

is limited. Compromises with the opposition are inevitable. The aforementioned lack of political will for gender sensitivity suggests that such compromises rarely come about.

Women's weak representation can, furthermore, be explained by inbuilt procedural and structural factors: Firstly, female candidates faced difficulties in the registration process of candidates, the organisation and funding of campaigns and were disadvantaged by the first-past-the-post election system.[39] Secondly, there are no local elections, but the lower administrative levels are led by appointed (mainly male) bureaucrats. Traditional chiefs are mostly men, too. Thus, women do not have opportunities to gain experience and prove their leadership qualities in political office. This reduces their chances of being nominated as candidates and being elected. Even if elected, women do not have the capacities to assert themselves as they lack the necessary skills and networks. Finally, cooperation among women is absent due to ethnic, class or party divisions. As these loyalties dominate over female solidarity, the influence of women in parliament is weakened and common initiatives

---

[37] The term *divided government* refers to a situation, where the party of the president does not control one or both chambers of the parliament. A variety of parties is represented in the Liberian parliament. See Appendix IV. National Elections Commission (NEC). *2005 Elections Results: Results by Political Party and Gender* [Website]. 2005. Available online at: http://www.necliberia.org/results/Senate/SenateByPPGender.html (Accessed on 30 August 2011); National Elections Commission (NEC). 2005 Elections Results: Results by Political Party and Gender [Website]. 2005. Available online at: http://www.necliberia.org/results/House/HouseByPPGender.html (Accessed on 30 August 2011).

[38] Shepherd, Laura J. 'Glossary'. In: ibid. (ed.). *Gender Matters in Global Politics. A Feminist Introduction to International Relations*. Abingdon, Routledge, 2010, p. xxi.

[39] British Broadcasting Corporation (BBC). *Liberia Country Profile* [Website]. 2010. Available online at: http://news.bbc.co.uk/1/hi/world/africa/country_profiles/1043500.stm (Accessed on 25 June 2011); Disney, Abigail E. & Reticker, Gini (dirs.). op. cit.; Fuest, Veronika, op. cit., p. 215; Kellow, Tim. op. cit., pp. 22-23; 'Women of Liberia's Mass Action for Peace'. In: *The Scavenger: Salvaging What's Left after the Masses Have Had Their Feed*. Undated. Available online at: http://www.thescavenger.net/people/women-of-liberias-mass-action-for-peace-37462-315.html (Accessed on 07 June 2012). The majority voting system discriminates against women.

are unlikely. Moreover, the voting of measures is only a first step, as they need to be implemented and respected.[40] Directly linked with this is the fact that women's participation must be fostered by measures in all of the domains examined above. Varying timeframes must be addressed, i.e. short-term actions in one sector must be supported by long-term, structural policies. For example, political participation of women has improved and can be advanced further by formally introducing and enforcing quotas.[41] But it is equally necessary to enable women to use these opportunities through better education and a change in societal attitudes towards female leadership. This is much more difficult to achieve and requires more time.[42] Similar connections obstruct rapid progress in other domains.

There is also a tendency to avoid societal tensions and conflicts in post-conflict Liberia. Women's empowerment contains conflict potential because it modifies gender relations, which can destabilise existing orders and even provoke the use of force. Consequently, one can say that the population adopts a pragmatic approach and gives priority to ideas providing for peace and stability at the expense of women's empowerment and gender equality. Similar attitudes already existed during the war, when the women's movement fought primarily for peace, while political and women's topics were not on the agenda, which limited their influence in these fields afterwards.[43]

All in all, there are certainly developments in favour of Liberian women, which are remarkable for a post-conflict society characterised by strong gender inequality.[44] Nevertheless, the substantial political, security, legal, socioeconomic and socio-cultural challenges and even negative external influences obstructing a gender-sensitive order are obvious.[45] In addition to this,

---

[40] Badmus, Alani. op. cit., p. 835; Bouta, Tsjeard et al. op. cit., pp. 74-74; Cook, Nikolas. op. cit., p. 7; ICG. op. cit., Liberia: Uneven Progress, p. 11; Kellow, Tim. op. cit., pp. 6, 15, 17, 25; Mehler, Andreas & Smith-Höhn, Judy. op. cit., p. 4.
[41] The 30 per cent quota of women was agreed to as an objective in the 2005 election. However, it is not formally established.
[42] Badmus, Alani. op. cit., pp. 834-835; Kellow, Tim. op. cit., pp. 7, 19-20, 23-24, 29.
[43] Allen, Bonnie. op. cit.
[44] See chapter 5.2. on positive, negative or absent repercussions of post-conflict settings on gender relations and women's empowerment.
[45] United Nations General Assembly. op. cit., Liberia Is Writing New History.

there are underlying factors relating to masculinity that prevent a more gender-sensitive social order that will be discussed in the following section.

6.2. The ubiquitous impact of masculinity and its relevance for gender sensitivity in the making and building of peace

Another less obvious and more abstract, but important obstacle for the creation of a gender sensitive post-conflict order is the influence of patterns of
masculinity. Their influence at multiple levels, the sub-state level (micro),
state (mezzo) and international (macro) level, is examined. This shift in terms
of levels of analysis is imperative in order to include external influences that
play a major role here.[46]

On the macro level, the male-dominated structures and policies of sub-
regional and international organisations had an impact in qualitative and
quantitative terms.[47] Despite their commitment to gender mainstreaming,
gender equality is often weak or absent.[48] At the decision-making and diplo-
matic level, staff of international organisations are predominantly male and
characterised by the masculine institutional culture,[49] which can even lead to
highly negative manifestations of masculinity such as sexual abuse. Besides,
the peace process was seen as a male or masculine domain and women
were not systematically integrated into it.[50] Equally problematic is the pres-

---

[46] Aboagye, Festus B. & Bah, Alhaji M. S. op. cit.; Aisha, Fatoumata. op. cit., pp. 147-163.
[47] In the introduction, quantitative and qualitative factors were defined as follows: "*Qualitative factors* refer to non-quantifiable domains and developments such as traditional
perceptions of gender and include policies regarding gender issues and outcomes of
policies. *Quantitative factors* subsume figure and proportions, for example the percentage of female members of parliament." See chapter 1.2.
[48] Bouta, Tsjeard et al. op. cit., p. 51; Harders, Cilja. 'Krieg und Frieden in internationalen
Beziehungen'. In: Rosenberger, Sieglinde & Sauer, Birgit (eds.). *Politikwissenschaft
und Geschlecht. Konzepte – Verknüpfungen – Perspektiven*. Wien, Facultas Verlag,
2004, pp. 230-231. For a definition of gender mainstreaming, see section 6.1. and
Shepherd, Laura J. op. cit., 'Glossary'.
[49] Women are not absent, but tend to concentrate in certain policy fields or at the administrative level.
[50] About the negotiations between the Liberian, Sierra Leonean and Guinean heads of
states that was realised by MARWOPNET, Brownell says: "[T]he greatest problem was
'the male mentality that says women are not supposed to be involved in these things'."
Brownell, Mary as quoted in African Women and Peace Support Group. op. cit., p. 46.

ence of masculinity in "governing principles"[51] and its qualitative influence on policies and their outcomes.[52] The Security Sector Reform and the Disarmament, Demobilisation, Rehabilitation and Reintegration process were, for example, organized in a male-focused way neglecting women's needs.[53] Although the external intervention has been more gender-sensitive than previous ones, these deficiencies regarding gender reveal in many respects how strongly rooted masculinity is in international structures. As the international and domestic spheres interact the inconsistent implementation of gender awareness and the clear presence of masculinity in the former had a considerable and negative influence on Liberia.[54]

Masculinity and patriarchy are also inherent on the state, i.e. mezzo level. In quantitative terms, women are marginalised or excluded from institutions or included in a merely patriarchal and essentialist way. As a result they are under-represented in all spheres of the state, especially at the decision-making level.[55] But qualitative aspects such as gender-sensitive measures and policy outcomes are important, too. Albeit Liberia is headed by a female president, the persistence and influence of masculinities is obvious as she is unlikely to considerably change her male-dominated environment, but rather risks being influenced and 'masculinised' by it herself, as the use of gender in the campaign has shown.[56] Women are largely absent from party structures despite

---

[51] Cockburn, Cynthia. 'The Continuum of Violence: A Gender Perspective on War and Peace'. In: Giles, Wenona & Hyndman, Jennifer (eds.). *Sites of Violence: Gender and Conflict Zones*. London, University of California Press, 2004, p. 29.

[52] Cockburn, Cynthia. op. cit., 'The Continuum of Violence', pp. 29-30; Zalewski, Marysia. 'Feminist International Relations: Making Sense...' In: Shepherd, Laura J. (ed.). *Gender Matters in Global Politics. A Feminist Introduction to International Relations*. Abingdon, Routledge, 2010, pp. 37-39.

[53] AI. op. cit., *Liberia: A Flawed Process*; ICG. op. cit., *Liberia: Uneven Progress*, p. 11-12.

[54] Caprioli, Mary. 'Gendered Conflict'. In: *Journal of Peace Research*, Vol. 37, No. 1, 2000, p. 55; Kellow. Tim. op. cit., p. 31. The deployment of a female-only police union by the UN shows that the influence of the international sphere relating to gender awareness can also be positive. See Cordel, Kristen. *Liberia: Women Peacekeepers and Human Security*. Open Democracy (8 October), 2009. Available online at: http://www.opendemocracy.net/blog/liberia/kristen-cordell/2009/10/08/liberia-women-peacekeepers-and-human-security (Accessed on 02 August 2011).

[55] Bouta, Tsjeard et al. op. cit., p. 51.

[56] African Women and Peace Support Group. op. cit., pp. 31, 55; Bouta, Tsjeard et al. op. cit., p. 62; Caprioli, Mary & Boyer, Mark A. 'Gender, Violence, and International Crisis'. In: *The Journal of Conflict Resolution*, Vol. 45, No. 4, 2001, pp. 507-508; 'Women of Liberia's Mass Action for Peace'. op. cit. See section 5.2.

formal commitments to improve their representation.[57] They also face gendered discrimination which can be explained by individual and structural features of masculinity, i.e. harassment by male colleagues before and during elections, and by procedural and structural disadvantages within the political system, such as the voting system or the centralised state.[58] In various ways, women's political participation is obstructed by masculine characteristics within the state. Even after having successfully entered the political arena, women in office face resistance from their male counterparts and are not treated as equals. Because of a lack of skills and experiences it is difficult for female politicians to enter political networks and influence processes. So it is arguable in how far Liberian women – if present – have effectively entered the political realm.[59]

On the micro level, e.g. on the community level or within families, masculinity as well as patriarchy persists in traditional hierarchical structures. These structures determine labour divisions; girls and women are expected to fulfil certain roles and tasks. Simultaneously, their access to education and resources are limited.[60]

A strong interdependence between the influences of masculinities at the micro, mezzo and macro level can be observed. The limitation of the majority of the female population by masculine values and practices on the micro level obstructs, for example, greater participation of women at the state level. However, even those women who successfully entered the political sphere are discriminated against by male colleagues. This is further negatively influenced by the international sphere.[61]

In addition to this cross-level interaction, there is strong path dependency, meaning the difficulties resulting from masculinity are hard to overcome, as its

---

[57] Kellow, Tim. op. cit., p. 5.
[58] See Bouta, Tsjeard et al. op. cit., p. 51; Connell, Raewyn W. *Masculinities*. Cambridge, Polity Press, 2005, p. xx; Kellow, Tim. op. cit., pp. 5-6, 15, 22, 24. See also Connell, Raewyn W. *Gender and Power: Society, the Person and Sexual Politics*. Cambridge, Polity Press, 1987, pp. 125-132.
[59] Kellow, Tim. op. cit., pp. 6, 22-23; 'Women of Liberia's Mass Action for Peace'. op. cit.
[60] Kellow, Tim. op. cit., p. 19.
[61] Aboagye, Festus B. & Bah, Alhaji M. S. op. cit.; Caprioli, Mary. op. cit., p. 55; Kellow. Tim. op. cit., p. 31.

underlying structures persist and are reproduced.[62] This obstructs developments towards greater gender sensitivity in the short term and underlines, why it is necessary to address structural factors.

The influence of masculinity on the emergence of gendered violence is another area that is to be considered.[63] In the theory chapter of this study, it was argued that there are relationships between masculinity and violence. Firstly, violent masculine behavioural patterns can result from violence.[64] Secondly, organisational cultures and structures promote violent masculinities. Both correlations can be observed in Liberia. Aggressive masculine behaviour is likely to be a consequence of violence given the intensity and duration of the civil war. Equally, one can observe that violent masculinities were created by organisational and institutional cultures, as gendered violence was used as a weapon of war and was a consequence of a lack of discipline. Hence, it was inherently present within state and rebel forces.[65] This explains why high levels of violence persisted after the fighting. At the same time, violence was difficult to address because social norms had eroded and the acceptance of violence increased. Altogether, one can conclude that violent tendencies became to some extent part of a hegemonic masculinity.

---

[62] Bouta, Tsjeard et al. op. cit., p. 51.

[63] See section 2.2. and Pankhurst, Donna. op. cit., 'Post-War Backlash Violence against Women', pp. 295-304; Pringle, Keith. 'Violence'. In: Flood, Michael et al. (eds.) *International Encyclopedia of Men and Masculinities*. London, Routledge, 2007, pp. 612-615. Gendered violence is a complex phenomenon and not exclusively caused by masculinities. They play, however, an influence in its emergence. Pankhurst, Donna. op. cit., 'Post-War Backlash Violence against Women', pp. 295-304.

[64] Connell, Raewyn W. *The Men and the Boys*. Cambridge, Polity Press, 2000, p. 224; Goldstein, Joshua S. *War and Gender*. Cambridge, Cambridge University Press, 2001, pp. 290-291, 293.

[65] Association of Female Lawyers of Liberia (AFELL) & The Editors. 'Hundreds of Victims Silently Grieving. In: Turshen, Meredeth & Twagiramariya, Clotilde (eds.). *What Women Do in Wartime*. London, Zed Books, 1998, pp. 129-137; Connell, Raewyn W. *Gender*. Cambridge, Polity Press, 2002, pp. 102-104; George, Kla Emmanuel Gamoe. *Women as Agents of Peace During the Civil Wars in Liberia and Sierra Leone, 1989—2005*. Undated. (Mimeographed Paper), pp. 1-2. Available online at: www.isud.typepad. com/files/george1.doc (Accessed on 28 April 2011); Hearn, Jeff. 'Violence, Organisational and Collective'. In: Flood, Michael et al. *International Encyclopedia of Men and Masculinities*. London, Routledge, 2007, p. 619; Pankhurst, Donna. 'Sexual Violence in War'. In: Shepherd, Laura J. (ed.). *Gender Matters in Global Politics. A Feminist Introduction to International Relations*. Abingdon, Routledge, 2010, p. 152. See also sections 2.2. and 4.1.

In addition, the theory chapter showed that masculine violence can be a reaction to modified gender relations.[66] These changes are drastic in post-war Liberia, where women's roles shifted in many ways. Hence, men tried to defend the patriarchal dividend or felt de-masculinised due to women's progress towards empowerment.[67] Especially ex-combatants risked suffering from or feeling a loss of their manhood after DDRR. Furthermore, women could not protect themselves from violence because of their difficult situation. These factors led to a high level of gendered violence.

All in all, this contemplation demonstrates the practical importance of influences of masculinities in relation to gender in peacebuilding. An understanding of the impacts is essential as they are present on various interdependent levels and obstruct greater gender sensitivity. Features of masculinity are also important for the emergence and consequently the prevention of violence in (post-)conflict settings.[68] Hence, existing challenges can only be addressed if aspects of masculinity are identified and integrated into approaches to solving the problems relating to gender.

6.3. Theoretical conclusions: Opportunities and challenges for a gender-sensitive peace

The analysis of the Liberian case has demonstrated that the theoretical claims about women in peacebuilding and ensuing gender sensitivity are – although desirable – difficult to implement. It is now necessary to discuss

---

[66] Alsop, Rachel; Fitzsimons, Annette & Lennon, Kathleen. *Theorizing Gender.* Cambridge, Polity Press, 2002, pp.134-135; Connell, Raewyn W. op. cit., *Masculinities*, pp. 82-84; 86-89; Connell, Raewyn W. *The Men and the Boys.* Cambridge, Polity Press, 2000, pp. 20-21, 217; Hamber, Brandon. 'Masculinity and Transitional Justice: An Exploratory Essay'. In: *The International Journal of Transitional Justice*, Vol. 1, 2007; pp. 384-385; Pankhurst, Donna. op. cit., 'Post-War Backlash Violence against Women', pp. 300, 303, 307, 311; Pillay, Anu. 'Violence against Women in the Aftermath'. In: Meintjes, Sheila; Pillay, Anu & Turshen, Meredeth (eds.). *The Aftermath: Women in Post-Conflict Transformation.* London, Zed Books, 2001, pp. 40-41; Seidler, Victor. Op. cit., pp. 66-67, 69; Whitehead, Stephen M. 'Patriarchal Dividend'. In: Flood, Michael et al. (eds.). *International Encyclopedia of Men and Masculinities.* London, Routledge, 2007, pp. 467-468.
[67] Hamber, Brandon. op. cit., pp. 384-385; Whitehead, Stephen M. op. cit., pp. 467-468.
[68] Connell, Raewyn W. op. cit., *Masculinities*, p. xviii.

what implications these findings have for gender theory in peacemaking and peacebuilding.

The participation of women in peacemaking and peacebuilding does indeed increase the probability that gender issues are addressed and integrated into policies after the conflict. However, this positive impact should not be taken for granted a priori, as gender sensitivity and equality meet a variety of hurdles provoking backlashes, as has been shown in the preceding analysis.[69] Hence, not only is it important that women participate in the peace process at all levels, but it is especially relevant how they do it. In relation to this, one has to review theoretical approaches and ask if they are not too strongly focused on quantitative aspects at the detriment of qualitative ones. The Liberian case made it obvious that women's movements suffer from inherent difficulties, such as a lack of cooperation, communication and consensus leading to the duplication of structures, inefficiency and finally the weakening of the movements.[70]

Women face discrimination and marginalisation in many different areas, such as the political, security, legal, socio-economic and socio-cultural, and at various levels. These are not separated, but interact. The example of increased political participation of women reveals that it can only be achieved if their marginalisation in education is equally addressed. Hence, changes in a specific domain and at the micro level can be prerequisite for developments on a larger political or organisational scale. This does not mean that there is necessarily a positive effect.[71] However, it highlights that advancements at one

[69] Bouta,Tsjeard et al. op. cit., pp. 52-55. See also Bop, Codou. 'Women in Conflicts, Their Gains and Their Losses'. In: Meintjes, Sheila; Pillay, Anu & Turshen, Meredeth (eds.). The Aftermath: Women in Post-Conflict Transformation. London, Zed Books, 2001, pp. 19-34; Meintjes, Sheila. 'War and Post-War Shifts in Gender Relations'. In: Meintjes, Sheila; Pillay, Anu & Turshen, Meredeth (eds.). The Aftermath: Women in Post-Conflict Transformation. London, Zed Books, 2001 pp. 63-77; Pankhurst, Donna. 'Introduction: Gendered War and Peace'. In: ibid. (ed.). Gendered Peace: Women's Struggles for Post-War Justice and Reconciliation. London, Routledge, 2008, pp. 1-30; Pankhurst, Donna. op. cit., 'Post-War Backlash Violence against Women', pp. 293-320; Pillay, Anu. op. cit., 'Violence against Women in the Aftermath', pp. 35-45.
[70] African Women and Peace Support Group. op. cit., p. 25, 32; Fleshman, Michael. op. cit.; Solomon, Christiana. op. cit., p. 178-179. See also Kellow, Tim. op. cit.
[71] Bouta, Tsjeard et al. op. cit., p. 55.

level often depend on and are only achievable in connection with changes on another level. Likewise, different timeframes, i.e. the short- and long-term, are also interdependent. Consequently, a more holistic approach is imperative that considers and analyses the existing interconnections, which should lead to a better understanding of both positive and negative post-conflict trends relating to gender.

These findings also have practical implications. The international community strongly favours women's participation in peace processes and, as a result, in post-conflict politics. This can, however, only be successfully realised, if external actors adjust their support mechanisms to the specific situation in an encompassing way and in the long run.[72]

Another aspect that is highly important for theories on gender in peacebuilding is the inclusion of masculinity studies. Although it is debatable, whether one should (re-)focus on men and masculinity within the context of gender and peace, this is in reality inevitable. Certainly, this should not be done in an essentialist way perceiving men as naturally violent and aggressive and women as their victims, but the agency of both genders plays an important role and can only be understood in relation to each other.[73] Thus, it is essential to consider that masculinity represents a ubiquitous and often structural obstacle for greater gender sensitivity within a society on the sub-state and state level, and influences it from the outside, too. The masculine character of the international system shows how persistent and influential masculinity is, as it remains intact despite the attempts to promote gender awareness and equality regarding personnel and policies. The difficulties to overcome influences of masculinity – as well as other structural challenges – are linked with path-dependency that tends to make changes within a society more difficult or impedes them even totally, because future developments are predetermined by existing structures and behavioural patterns.[74] Positive devel-

---

[72] Aisha, Fatoumata. op. cit., p. 149.
[73] Cohn, Carol & Enloe, Cynthia. 'A Conversation with Cynthia Enloe: Feminists Look at Masculinity and the Men Who Wage War'. In: *Signs*, Vol. 28, No. 4, 2003, pp. 1188, 1199; Goldstein, Joshua S. op. cit.; Hamber, Brandon. op. cit., pp. 379, 383, 387; Pillay, Anu. op. cit., 'Violence against Women in the Aftermath', p. 41.
[74] Pierson, Paul. 'Increasing Returns, Path Dependence, and the Study of Politics'. In: *The American Political Science Review*, Vol. 94, No. 2, 2000, p. 252; Schultze, Rainer-

opment is therefore unlikely unless underlying patterns and structures can be successfully modified.

Moreover, violence is predominantly resorted to by men, so that aspects of masculinity are important to understand and prevent post-conflict violence. As the latter is a major threat to a gender-sensitive order and embraces much more than merely physical assaults, the research that is done on relations of masculinity and violence should be integrated into findings on women in peacebuilding.[75] All in all, post-conflict backlashes can in many respects only be adequately analysed and apprehended against the background of masculinity patterns, including patriarchy.

Finally, it is important to question the normative component of the theoretical approaches on women in peacebuilding. Gender theory, including literature about women and peace is often strongly based on Western concepts and principles.[76] Thus, it is difficult or even impossible to transfer them to non-occidental contexts. Moreover, radical changes are unlikely to occur in a society that is deeply influenced by gender inequality and patriarchy. Furthermore, the masculine character of the international community contradicts the very norms,[77] it tries to promote and risks rendering them incredible. Hence, more flexible, realistic and adaptable approaches are necessary.

In this context, one must also consider the specific nature of post-conflict societies. The Liberian case study uncovered pragmatism as well as the tendency to avoid controversies and tensions within the society in order to prevent another outbreak of violent conflict in the still fragile country.[78] Therefore, there is clearly a trade-off between peace, security and stability on the one

Olaf. 'Pfadabhängigkeit'. In: Nohlen, Dieter & Schultze, Rainer-Olaf (eds.). *Lexikon der Politikwissenschaft: Theorien, Methoden, Begriffe: Band 1 & 2.* München, Verlag C.H. Beck, 2004, pp. 683-384.

[75] See, for example, Connell, Raewyn W. op. cit., *The Men and the Boys*, pp. 213-215; Pankhurst, Donna. op. cit., 'Post-War Backlash Violence against Women'.

[76] Ramsbotham, Oliver; Woodhouse, Tom & Miall, Hugh. *Contemporary Conflict Resolution: The Prevention, Management and Transformation of Deadly Conflicts.* Cambridge, Polity Press, 2005, pp. 265-274; Väyrynen, Tarja. 'Gender and Peacebuilding'. In: Richmond, Oliver P. (ed.) *Palgrave Advances in Peacebuilding: Critical Developments and Approaches.* Basingstoke, Palgrave Macmillan, 2010, pp. 137-153.

[77] Jones, Adam. 'Does 'Gender' Make the World Go Round? Feminist Critiques of International Relations'. In: *Review of International Studies,* No. 22, 1996, p. 408.

[78] Disney, Abigail E. & Reticker, Gini (dirs.). op. cit. See also section 4.3.

hand and gender sensitivity and women's empowerment on the other.[79] This is understandable considering the traumatisation of the conflict-ridden population. Furthermore, it might even prevent women from a stronger set-back, which they risk suffering from in case of another conflict.[80]

Adjustments towards more flexibility are equally required regarding the evaluation of outcomes. Here, normativity should be combined with an adapted theoretical framework, which allows evaluating positive or negative developments concerning the societal status of women against the respective socio-cultural background. As a result, the ideal of gender sensitivity would be maintained, but it would be of a less absolute nature. Changes in gender relations could be specifically assessed in the social context of the country in question. This would avoid that discrimination against women was accepted or even justified. It would also allow identifying even seemingly minor achievements, which are considerable for societies with a gender-insensitive tradition. Furthermore, cultural sensitivity in relation with gender in peacemaking and peacebuilding would prevent accusations that gender theories are Western-orientated or even neo-imperialist and hence increase their acceptance.[81]

In sum, the multi-level and multi-factorial analysis of the Liberian case helped to combine theoretical approaches regarding gender in peace processes and post-conflict settings by including masculinity theory into assumptions about women in peacemaking and peacebuilding. Not only is this theoretically relevant, but it is also of practical importance in other regions of the world because it allows for the conceptualisation of more adequate strategies aiming

---

[79] Connell, Raewyn W. op. cit., *Masculinities*, pp. 82-84, 86-89; Hamber, Brandon. op. cit., pp. 384-385; Pankhurst, Donna. op. cit., 'Post-War Backlash Violence against Women', pp. 300, 303, 307, 311; Pillay, Anu. op. cit., 'Violence against Women in the Aftermath', pp. 40-41; Seidler, Victor. 'Masculinity and Violence'. In: May, Larry et al. (eds.). *Rethinking Masculinity: Philosophical Explorations in Light of Feminism*. London, Rowman & Littlefield, 1996, pp. 66-67, 69; Whitehead, op. cit., pp. 467-468.

[80] Meintjes, Sheila. op. cit., pp. 63-77; Pankhurst, Donna. op. cit., 'Introduction', p. 8, pp. 1-30; Pankhurst, Donna. op. cit., 'Post-War Backlash Violence against Women', pp. 293-320; Pillay, Anu. op. cit., 'Violence against Women in the Aftermath', pp. 35-45. See also sections 2.2. and 4.3.

[81] See Agathangelou, Anna M. & Turcotte, Heather M. 'Postcolonial Theories and Challenges to 'First World-ism''. In: Shepherd, Laura J. (ed.). *Gender Matters in Global Politics: A Feminist Introduction to International Relations*. Abingdon, Routledge, 2010, pp. 44-58; Kellow, Tim. op. cit.

at effectively improving the situation of women and avoiding backlashes after conflicts.

7. Conclusion

For almost two decades, Liberia attracted attention because of the atrocious intra-state war it experienced. In this hostile and deadly environment, Liberian women worked from the very beginning of the conflict with non-violent means for its end. Their commitment contributed decisively to the final signing of a peace accord, which ended the violence and allowed for the beginning of the reconstruction of the country. But did it create 'real' peace, especially for those who asked for it most ardently, i.e. Liberian women? For many of them, it seems, nothing is definitely won, but the on-going neglect of their needs and the

> "lack of representation is equivalent to the denial of one of [their] fundamental rights: the right to be seen, be heard and be counted."[1]

As literature on gender in peacebuilding claims that the participation of women in peace processes leads to sustainable, gender-sensitive peace, the question asked in the introduction was: To what extent has the role of women in the Liberian peacemaking and peacebuilding contributed to gender-sensitive outcomes in post-conflict Liberian society? Based on a definition of gender-sensitive peace, this study analysed the gender sensitivity of the Liberian post-conflict order in qualitative and quantitative terms by reference to a specially conceived analytical framework. Positive and negative post-conflict developments in the political, security, legal, socio-economic and socio-cultural sphere were assessed on the micro, mezzo and macro level of Liberian society. External influences such as post-conflict DDRR measures of the UN were also regarded. In addition, obstacles to gender sensitivity such as internal difficulties of organisations and adverse impacts of masculinities on Liberian society were identified and evaluated.

As a result, the analysis identified achievements in the political, security, legal, socio-economic and socio-cultural domains such as the strong presence

---

[1] African Women and Peace Support Group. *Liberian Women Peacemakers: Fighting for the Right to Be Seen, Heard, and Counted.* Trenton, Africa World Press, 2004, p. 27.

of female politicians in the government including the presidency.[2] These were respectable as Liberian society is historically marked by gender inequality and faces enormous difficulties caused by the conflict and its repercussions. On balance, this progress was outweighed by quantitative and qualitative challenges on all levels and in all spheres, for example the persistence of customary law discriminating against women. Hence, the participation of Liberian women's organisations in peacemaking and peacebuilding contributed to the ending of the conflict. But beyond that, it led to a limited extent to a gender-sensitive peace at the micro, mezzo and macro level of post-conflict Liberian society, as real empowerment of women was not achieved.[3]

The study has also identified obstacles explaining why deficiencies regarding gender sensitivity persist. Firstly, internal difficulties of women's organisations such as a lack of cooperation due to political and ethnic allegiances, difficulties in terms of funding and insufficient experience and capacities of women active in the movements limited the influence of the organisations. Secondly, the study uncovered interdependences of factors in different domains and at various levels impeding greater gender inclusiveness. For example, poor education of girls is connected with economic dependence of women or difficulties to enter the political arena. This implies that measures taken in one area aiming at challenges at a specific level are inefficient, as they fail to address connected or underlying issues. Thus, a holistic approach is required in order to overcome complex structures of interdependent obstacles. Thirdly, collective, individual and structural influences of certain masculinities on the substate, state and international level represent hurdles to gender inclusion. Features of masculinity also contribute to the emergence of violence. However, it is too early to fully appreciate the degree of gender-sensitivity in post-conflict Liberia because many problems are structural, pre-conflict patterns or based on traditional values. As these are socially entrenched, it will take several generations to achieve greater gender equality.

It was further highlighted that 'women' are not a monolithic group. Depending on ethnicity, age, class or location, women had varying experiences in the

---

[2] See Appendix III.
[3] African Women and Peace Support Group. op. cit., p. 56.

conflict and participated in different ways – as victims, combatants and peacemakers at the grassroots or political level. Differentiation is also important regarding the notion of gender sensitivity because there are not only differences between men and women, but also differences within a gender. Advantages and inconveniences vary for Liberian women according to their individual social and economic situation, as the example of female Americo-Liberians shows who have greater opportunities than the majority of rural, poorly educated women – and even many Liberian men.

The conclusions drawn have an impact on the design of policies of donors. It is imperative that external actors promoting gender sensitivity in post-conflict settings have encompassing knowledge of the history and particularities of the respective conflict in order to be able to efficiently and sustainably include gender issues into their policies. Besides, the participation of women in peace processes can have adverse effects on the objective of creating gender sensitivity in the aftermath of a conflict. Hence, not only should women be central, but men and their concerns must be integrated into strategies, too, in order to counterbalance potential negative outcomes that are due to reactive responses by the male population as a consequence of shifts in gender relations. Furthermore, national orders can be seen as mirrors of the international level. If structures and policies of external actors such as the UN are gender-insensitive or predominantly masculine, their impact on post-conflict countries risks obstructing positive developments regarding gender sensitivity as they do not serve as a model for their very policies.[4] Hence, stakeholders should recognise that due to their characteristics they risk wielding negative influence on a country they intervene in. Not only does this have adverse consequences for women in the respective country, but it contradicts the objectives and values of the international community. Measures and expectations should further be adjusted to local contexts in order to avoid inadequate poli-

---

[4] See section 5.2. and African Women and Peace Support Group. op. cit., p. 46; Bouta, Tsjeard et al. *Gender, Conflict, and Development*. Washington D.C., The World Bank, 2005, p. 51; Cohn, Carol & Enloe, Cynthia. 'A Conversation with Cynthia Enloe: Feminists Look at Masculinity and the Men Who Wage War'. In: *Signs*, Vol. 28, No. 4, 2003, pp. 1198-1199, 1204; Harders, Cilja. 'Krieg und Frieden in internationalen Beziehungen'. In: Rosenberger, Sieglinde & Sauer, Birgit (eds.). *Politikwissenschaft und Geschlecht. Konzepte – Verknüpfungen – Perspektiven*. Wien, Facultas Verlag, 2004, pp. 230-231.

cies and the imposition of Western concepts at the expense of more urgent problems.[5] These results do not reduce the relevance of women's participation in peacemaking and peacebuilding; neither do they negate the significance of gender-sensitive peace. In effect, together with the fact that "it is much easier to talk of transformation than to achieve it",[6] it is highlighted that the realisation of such a post-conflict social order depends on much more than the mere inclusion of women in the peace process, which is, nevertheless, a first – although potentially dangerous – step forward.

The present work connected the discourse concerning the allegedly positive effect of women in peacemaking and peacebuilding with a theoretical evaluation of women's activities and their consequences in Liberia. The analysis of one country case cannot entirely fill the knowledge gap that exists in relation to the question why (African) women are unable to maintain leadership positions, but suffer from backlashes after conflicts.[7] Nonetheless, the approach is useful to comprehensively illuminate specific aspects of the problem examined in a particular context and intensively discuss them.[8] It elucidated multidimensional and multi-level interdependence between factors obstructing gender sensitive. Connections between problems are better understood and can therefore be addressed more effectively. The inclusion of masculinity theory underlined the importance of influences of masculinity on the micro, mezzo, and macro level as well as the need to include men and masculinities into post-conflict policies aiming at gender sensitivity.

Future research should continue exploring impacts of masculinities in order to identify possibilities to address challenges emanating from them. Furthermore, it is imperative to more strongly integrate local perceptions of gender, gender sensitivity and masculinity that exist in (post-)conflict countries, because theoretical perceptions and policies are too often culturally insensitive and dominated by Western ideas. This would allow to adjust both the notion

---

[5] See section 5.3.
[6] Cooper, Etweda as quoted in African Women and Peace Support Group. op. cit., p. 56.
[7] Bop, Codou as quoted in Bouta, Tsjeard et al. *Gender, Conflict, and Development.* Washington D.C., The World Bank, 2005, p. 55.
[8] Landman, Todd. *Issues and Methods in Comparative Politics: An Introduction.* London, Routledge, 2003, p. 34.

of gender sensitivity as well as policies to the respective local context and to local requirements without ignoring more pressing problems. Finally, the notion of gender sensitivity should be re-considered aiming at greater equality not only between 'men' and 'women', but also between privileged and disadvantaged population groups regardless of their genders.

8. Appendix

8.1. Appendix I: Map of the Republic of Liberia

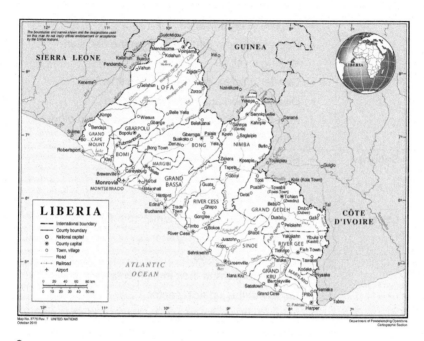

Source:
United Nations, Department of Peacekeeping Operations, Cartographic Section,
Map No. 3775 Rev.7, October 2010.

8.2. Appendix II: Analytical framework

AREA	INDICATORS
Political	• Participation (voting) • Degree of organisation • Representation, participation on the decision-making level • Gender policies and their implementation • Discrimination against women by the male/masculine character of the state and other relevant collective bodies
Security	• Security Sector Reform • DDRR programmes • Physical security for women
Legal	• Women's rights (e.g. inheritance rights, property rights) • Gender bias of laws • Legal reforms and their implementation • Quality of the juridical sector • Impunity of gendered crimes during and after the conflict
Socio-economic/ Socio-cultural	• Informal/formal employment (access to the job market) • Economic/financial (in)dependence • Land rights, inheritance • Norms, values, traditions • Education, training opportunities, skills • Labour division, gender roles within the family • Gendered/domestic violence, rape • Persistence of traditional/customary social structures and practices (e.g. female genital mutilation)

AREA	INDICATORS
External	<ul><li>Inclusion or neglect of gender issues in resolutions, policies, missions and training</li><li>Gender equality within the deployed staff, creation of institutions responsible for gender issues</li><li>Support or neglect of women's participation in the peace process by external actors, actual participation of women in the (formal) peace process</li><li>Other forms of promotion of women's participation</li><li>Implementation and respect of gender awareness by external actors themselves</li></ul>
Procedural	<ul><li>Peace process</li><li>Lack of capacities, internal deficiencies</li><li>Actual targets (ambitious, pragmatist)</li><li>Relations/divisions between different women's movements</li><li>Relations of women with external agents,</li><li>External influence (positive/negative), external support of activities of women's organisations</li><li>Male institutions</li></ul>

Area	Level	Advances	Challenges
POLITICAL			
	Micro	increased participation of women in elections, women make up over 50% of the registered voters (2005)	
	Mezzo	increase in women's participation in civil society organisations (creation of women's organisations in various socio-political areas, gender equity within organisations)	centralised governmental system: no local elections; mainly male elders and chiefs (no opportunities for women to gain experience and to prove leadership qualities)
			registration process for candidacy discriminates against women
			women face difficulties in leading and funding campaigns
			female candidates and politicians are discriminated against by male colleagues
	Macro	female president	
		strong representation of women in the cabinet (30%) and other key offices and positions	
		creation of Gender and Development ministry (2001)	Gender and Development ministry lacks capacities and staff
		30% quota for female candidates	quota is only informally agreed and not met; only weak representation of women in both chambers
		creation of the Truth and Reconciliation Commission foreseen by the CPA	its gender sensitivity was - although better compared to other TRCs in post-conflict countries - unsatisfactory
			former warlords responsible for human rights violations are members of parliament
		commitment of the government to integrate gender into all policies	
			first-past-the-post voting system disadvantages women
			women lack experience, capacity and network in order to work effectively in parliament

Area	Level	Advances	Challenges
SECURITY			
	Micro		persistent high level of gender-based violence and abuse (e.g. discrimination, physical/sexual assaults and abuse); tolerance of violent behaviour
			FGM is persistently and increasingly practised (no law against FGM)
	Mezzo		violent behaviour is facilitated by various factors (e.g. availability and circulation of SALW, lack of infrastructure, erosion of moral norms and social constraints during the conflict)
		creation of women and children protection units, community policing, and county attorneys	female ex-combatants face marginalisation and stigmatisation at their return to the communities (precarious, unsecure living conditions, no social support network)
	Macro	SSR (including the army, police and other security forces) aims at integrating women into the security sector and at increasing their numbers: - army: 5% women; - police: ca. 12% women	initially targeted percentage (20%) of women in the security forces was not achieved
		training includes issues on gender issues, rule of law and human rights	insufficient training especially concerning gender issues
			national security remains fragile and dependent on external actors
		participation of women and girls in the DDRR process (21% women, 2% girls)	many eligible women could not participate in the DDRR or dropped out previously
			women were insufficiently integrated into the planning and implementation of DDRR by the responsible actors
			lack of female personnel and knowledge concerning gender within the responsible organisations
		attempts to adjust DDRR to requirements of both genders	insufficient funding, women's needs were not met, lack of gender-specific information necessary to conceptualise a gender-sensitive DDRR

109

Area	Level	Advances	Challenges
LEGAL			
	Micro		women lack access to justice institutions (e.g. because of their illiteracy, fear or a lack of (financial) means)
	Mezzo	creation of county attorneys, better treatment and protection of victims	insufficient well-educated staff, juridical institutions are weakly present or absent in rural areas
			especially in rural areas, customary law dominates
		education concerning human and women's rights, increasing awareness of these issues	traditional practices and beliefs remain strong
	Macro	constitution interdicts discrimination	specific regulations in terms of gender-based discrimination are missing
		on-going review of constitution in order to render it more gender sensitive and inclusive	
		adjustments in the statutory law, e.g. 'inheritance law', 'rape law': women's status relating to inheritance, property, custody and sexual violence is improved	legal dualism: co-existence of customary and statutory law; persistence of customary deprives girls and women of important rights and leaves them vulnerable and dependent
		examination and review of all the laws concerning gender biases	
			culture of impunity

Area	Level	Advances	Challenges
SOCIO-CULTURAL / SOCIO-ECONOMIC	**Micro**		discrimination against girls and women because of religious, traditional and cultural practices
			high maternal and child mortality rate; women (e.g. rape victims) suffer from psychological consequences of the conflict (e.g. traumatisation)
			traditional role patterns and labour division persist; women are economically dependent on men and strongly underrepresented in certain sectors and the formal economy
			limited economic opportunities for women because of a lack of education, qualification and skills; economic marginalisation and dependence
			disproportional activity of women in certain sectors (e.g. agriculture) and informal economy
			limited access to material and immaterial resources (e.g. loans, land, property)
			high illiteracy rate among women
			lack of self-confidence and self-belief
	Mezzo	increase in female enrolment; policies to promote girls' education further and reduce their drop out rate; government policies aiming at reducing women's economic dependence	girls' enrolment remains lower than boys' (especially in high schools); drop-out of girls remains a problem
	Macro		external debts and scarce financial resources limit the scope of manoeuvre of the government
			insufficient health care facilities; women's health needs are not met

EXTERNAL	Advances	Challenges
International / sub-regional	UNSC resolutions include gender issues	little achievements by the Office of a Gender Advisor; climited reach; success of the office is limited in relation to its budget
	operational framework of the UNMIL includes a gender unit and an Office of a Gender Advisor; attempts to include gender mainstreaming in the mission	
	sensitisation of deployed civilian and military staff concerning sexual exploitation and gender issues	sexual exploitation and human rights abuses by peacekeeping forces (e.g. ECOMOG, UNMIL); insufficient training regarding gender issues
	certain acknowledgement of women's activism: women's organisations could present their positional paper at an ECOWAS meeting	
	MARWOPNET was allowed to participate in the peace talks in Ghana and signed the CPA	women's movements were not sufficiently recognised and allowed to participate in the formal peace process (e.g. by ECOWAS)
	after having been neglected at the beginning, women were finally integrated into the organisation of the DDRR process	initially, women did not participate in the planning and implementation od the DDRR
	to some extent, gender issues were taken into account and implemented in DDRR and SSR	conceptualisation of SSR and DDRR as technical projects: socio-political aspects and issues of human security and human rights were neglected
		practical problems in the implementation of DDRR (e.g. insufficient funding, lack of female staff and knowledge) to the detriment of eligible women and girls
	the UNMIL is considered to be more gender sensitive than other UN interventions	
	promotion of gender issues by external support for women's organisations	external support is non-sustainable and mainly directed at organisations corresponding to Western ideas regarding gender

8.4. Appendix IV: Distribution of seats in parliament (2005)

a) House of Representatives

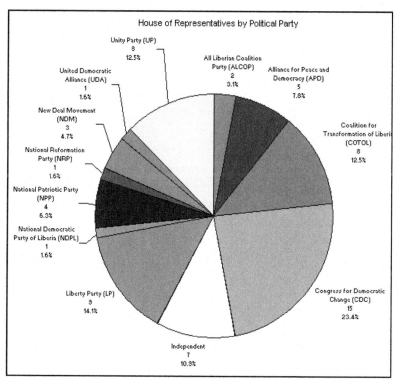

House of Representatives by Political Party

Unity Party (UP)
8
12.5%

All Liberian Coalition
Party (ALCOP)
2
3.1%

Alliance for Peace and
Democracy (APD)
5
7.8%

United Democratic
Alliance (UDA)
1
1.6%

New Deal Movement
(NDM)
3
4.7%

Coalition for
Transformation of Liberia
(COTOL)
8
12.5%

National Reformation
Party (NRP)
1
1.6%

National Patriotic Party
(NPP)
4
6.3%

National Democratic
Party of Liberia (NDPL)
1
1.6%

Liberty Party (LP)
9
14.1%

Congress for Democratic
Change (CDC)
15
23.4%

Independent
7
10.9%

Source:
National Elections Commission (NEC). *2005 Elections Results: Results by Political Party and Gender* [Website]. 2005. Available online at: http://www.necliberia.org/results/House/HouseByPPGender.html

113

Party	in %	No. of seats
All Liberian Coalition Party (ALCOP)	3.1%	2
Alliance for Peace and Democracy (APD)	7.8%	5
Coalition for Transformation of Liberia (COTOL)	12.5%	8
Congress for Democratic Change (CDC)	23.4%	15
Independent	10.9%	7
Liberty Party	14.1%	9
National Democratic Party of Liberia (NDPL)	1.6%	1
National Patriotic Party (NPP)	6.3%	4
National Reformation Party (NRP)	1.6%	1
New Deal Movement (NDM)	4.7%	3
United Democratic Alliance (UDA)	1.6%	1
Unity Party (UP)[1]	12.5%	8
Total	**100.1%**	**64**

---

[1] Party of Ellen Johnson-Sirleaf.

b) Senate

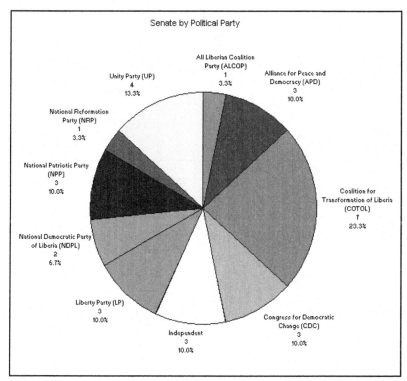

Senate by Political Party

All Liberian Coalition Party (ALCOP)
1
3.3%

Alliance for Peace and Democracy (APD)
3
10.0%

Unity Party (UP)
4
13.3%

National Reformation Party (NRP)
1
3.3%

National Patriotic Party (NPP)
3
10.0%

Coalition for Transformation of Liberia (COTOL)
7
23.3%

National Democratic Party of Liberia (NDPL)
2
6.7%

Liberty Party (LP)
3
10.0%

Independent
3
10.0%

Congress for Democratic Change (CDC)
3
10.0%

Source:
National Elections Commission (NEC). *2005 Elections Results: Results by Political Party and Gender* [Website]. 2005. Available online at: http://www.necliberia.org/results/Senate/SenateByPPGender.html

Party	in %	No. of seats
All Liberian Coalition Party (ALCOP)	3.3%	1
Alliance for Peace and Democracy (APD)	10%	3
Coalition for Transformation of Liberia (COTOL)	23.3%	7
Congress for Democratic Change (CDC)	10%	3
Independent	10%	3
Liberty Party	10%	3
National Democratic Party of Liberia (NDPL)	6.7%	2
National Patriotic Party (NPP)	10%	3
National Reformation Party (NRP)	3.3%	1
Unity Party (UP)	13.3%	4
Total	**99.9%**	**30**

9. Bibliography

Aboagye, Festus B. & Bah, Alhaji M. S. *Liberia at a Crossroads: A Preliminary Look at the United Nations Mission in Liberia (UNMIL) and the Protection of Civilians.* Pretoria, Institute of Security Studies (Occasional Paper No. 95), 2004. Available online at: http://www.iss.org.za/pubs/papers/95/Paper95.htm (Accessed on 28 June 2011).

Aboagye, Festus & Bah, Alahji M. S. (eds.). *A Tortuous Road to Peace: The Dynamics of Regional, UN and International Humanitarian Interventions in Liberia.* Pretoria, Publications of the Institute of Security Studies, 2005.

Ackerman, Ruthie. 'Rebuilding Liberia: One Brick at a Time'. In: *World Policy Journal*, Vol. 26, No. 2, 2009, pp. 83-92.

Adams, Melinda. 'Liberia's Election of Ellen Johnson-Sirleaf and Women's Executive Leadership in Africa'. In: *Politics & Gender*, Vol. 4, No. 3, 2008, pp. 475-484.

Adebajo, Adekeye. *Building Peace in West Africa: Liberia, Sierra Leone, and Guinea-Bissau.* London, Lynne Rienner Publishers, 2002.

Adebajo, Adekeye. *Liberia's Civil War: Nigeria, ECOMOG, and Regional Security in West Africa.* London, Lynne Rienner Publishers, 2002.

Adebajo, Adekeye. 'West Africa's Tragic Twins. Building Peace in Liberia and Sierra Leone'. In: Keating, Tom & Knight, W. Andy (eds.). *Building Sustainable Peace.* Edmonton, University of Alberta Press, 2004, pp. 167-188.

African Election Database. *Elections in Liberia* [Website]. 2011. Available online at: http://africanelections.tripod.com/lr.html#1997_Presidential_Election (Accessed on 04 May 2012).

African Women and Peace Support Group. *Liberian Women Peacemakers: Fighting for the Right to Be Seen, Heard, and Counted.* Trenton, Africa World Press, 2004.

Afrol News. *Gender Profile: Liberia* [Website]. Undated. Available online at: www.afrol.com/Categories/Women/profiles/liberia_women.htm (Accessed on 21 July 2011).

Afrol News. *UNMIL Sex Abuse Declines* [Website]. Undated. Available online at: http://www.afrol.com/articles/27647 (Accessed on 28 July 2011).

Agathangelou, Anna M. & Turcotte, Heather M. 'Postcolonial Theories and Challenges to 'First World-ism''. In: Shepherd, Laura J. (ed.). *Gender Matters in Global Politics: A Feminist Introduction to International Relations.* Abingdon, Routledge, 2010, pp. 44-58.

Aisha, Fatoumata. 'Mainstreaming Gender in Peace Support Operations: The United Nations Mission in Liberia'. In: Aboagye, Festus & Bah, Alahji (eds.). *A Tortuous Road to Peace: The Dynamics of Regional, UN and International Humanitarian Interventions in Liberia.* Pretoria, Publications of the Institute of Security Studies, 2005, pp. 147-163.

Alison, Miranda H. *Women and Political Violence: Female Combatants in Ethno-national Conflicts.* Abingdon, Routledge, 2009.

Allen, Bonnie. *Liberia: Paper Rights Flimsy Protection* [Website]. Nobel Peace Prize for African Women, 2010. Available online at: http://www.noppaw.net/?p=938pdf (Accessed on 25 July 2011).

Alsop, Rachel; Fitzsimons, Annette & Lennon, Kathleen. *Theorizing Gender.* Cambridge, Polity Press, 2002.

Amnesty International (AI). *Rwanda: "Marked for Death", Rape Survivors Living with HIV/AIDS in Rwanda.* 2004. Available online at: http://www.amnesty.org/en/library/asset/AFR47/007/2004/en/53d74ceb-d5f7-11dd-bb24-1fb85fe8fa05/afr470072004en.pdf (Accessed on 23 June 2011).

Amnesty International (AI). *Liberia: A Flawed Process Discriminates against Women and Girls.* 2008. Available online at: http://www.amnesty.org/en/library/asset/AFR34/004/2008/en/c075d220-00cf-11dd-a9d5-b31ac3ea5bcc/afr340042008eng.pdf (Accessed on 04 July 2011).

Amnesty International (AI). *Lessons from Liberia: Reintegrating Women in Postconflict Liberia.* 2009. Available online at: http://www.amnesty.org/en/library/asset/AFR34/002/2009/en/442e0181-c8e2-4057-81f6-d19ceddf0045/afr340022009en.pdf (Accessed on 28 June 2011).

Anderlini, Sanam Naraghi. *Women at the Peace Table: Making a Difference.* New York, United Nations Development Fund for Women, 2000.

118

Aning, Emmanuel Kwesi. *Managing Regional Security in West Africa: Ecowas, Ecomog and Liberia*. Copenhagen, Centre for Development Research (Working Paper No. 94.2), 1994.

Aning, Emmanuel Kwesi. 'Peacekeeping under ECOMOG: A Sub-regional Approach'. In: Cilliers, Jakkie & Mills, Greg (eds.). *From Peacekeeping to Complex Emergencies: Peace Support Missions in Africa*. Johannesburg, South African Institute of International Affairs, 1999, pp. 75-95.

Association of Female Lawyers of Liberia (AFELL) & The Editors. 'Hundreds of Victims Silently Grieving. In: Turshen, Meredeth & Twagiramariya, Clotilde (eds.). *What Women Do in Wartime*. London, Zed Books, 1998, pp. 129-137.

Badmus, Alani. 'Explaining Women's Roles in the West African Tragic Triplet: Sierra Leone, Liberia, and Cote d'Ivoire in Comparative Perspective'. In: *Journal of Alternative Perspectives in the Social Sciences*, Vol. 1, No. 3, 2009, pp. 808-839.

Baksh, Rawwida. 'Gender Mainstreaming in Post-conflict Reconstruction'. In Baksh, Rawwida et al. (eds.). *Gender Mainstreaming in Conflict Transformation: Building Sustainable Peace*. London, Commonwealth Secretariat, 2005, pp. 82-98.

Baksh, Rawwida et al. (eds.). *Gender Mainstreaming in Conflict Transformation: Building Sustainable Peace*. London, Commonwealth Secretariat, 2005.

Bannon, Ian & Correia, Maria C. (eds.). *The Other Half of Gender: Men's Issues in Development*. Washington D.C., The World Bank, 2006.

Barker, Gary & Ricardo, Christine. *Young Men and the Construction of Masculinity in Sub-Saharan Africa: Implications for HIV/AIDS, Conflict, and Violence*. Washington D.C., The World Bank (Social Development Papers: Conflict Prevention and Reconstruction, No. 26), 2005. Available online at: http://www.hsrc.ac.za/Document-86.phtml (Accessed on 18 August 2011).

Barnes, Elisabeth. *Agents for Change: Civil Society Roles in Preventing War and Building Peace*. Den Haag, European Centre for Conflict Prevention, International Secretariat of the Global Partnership for the Prevention of Armed Conflict (Issue Paper No. 2), 2006. Available online at: http://www.gppac.net/documents/GPPAC/Research/Issue_papers_200 6_-_2007_/2_Agents_for_Change.pdf (Accessed on 02 May 2011).

Bekoe, Dorina & Parajon, Christina. *Women's Role in Liberia's Reconstruction* [Website]. Washington D.C., United States Institute for Peace, 2007. Available online at: http://www.usip.org/publications/women-s-role-liberia-s-reconstruction (Accessed on 20 August 2011).

Benner, Thorsten & Blume, Till. 'A Second Chance for Liberia: President Johnson-Sirleaf's Quest to Build a New Liberia'. In: *Internationale Politik - Global Edition*, No. 9, 2008, pp. 40-45.

Bennett, Olivia et al. (eds.). *Arms to Fight, Arms to Protect: Women Speak out about Conflict*. London, Panos, 1995.

Bird's-eye View of Liberian History and Government [Website]. Undated. Available online at: http://www.africawithin.com/tour/liberia/hist_gov1.htm (Accessed on 28 August 2011).

Bonacker, Thorsten (ed.) *Sozialwissenschaftliche Konflikttheorien: Eine Einführung*. Wiesbaden, VS Verlag für Wissenschaften, 2008.

Bop, Codou. 'Women in Conflicts, Their Gains and Their Losses'. In: Meintjes, Sheila; Pillay, Anu & Turshen, Meredeth (eds.). *The Aftermath: Women in Post-Conflict Transformation*. London, Zed Books, 2001, pp. 19-34.

Bouta, Tsjeard et al. *Gender, Conflict, and Development*. Washington D.C., The World Bank, 2005.

Boutros-Ghali, Boutros. *An Agenda for Peace: Preventive Diplomacy, Peacemaking and Peace-keeping* [Website]. New York, United Nations, 1992. Available online at: http://www.un.org/Docs/SG/agpeace.html (Accessed on 18 August 2011).

Burnet, Jennie E. 'Gender Balance and the Meaning of Women in Governance in Post-Genocide Rwanda'. In: *African Affairs*, Vol. 107, No. 428, 2008, pp. 361-386.

British Broadcasting Corporation (BBC). *Liberia Country Profile* [Website]. 2010. Available online at: http://news.bbc.co.uk/1/hi/world/africa/country_profiles/1043500.stm (Accessed on 18 June 2011).

Buikema, Rosemarie & Smelik, Anneke. *Women's Studies and Culture: A Feminist Introduction*. London, Zed Books, 1993.

Cambridge Dictionaries Online [Website]. Cambridge, Cambridge University Press, 2011. Available online at: http://dictionary.cambridge.org/ (Accessed on 25 August 2011).

Cantrell, Tania H. & Bachmann, Ingrid. 'Who Is the Lady in the Window? A Comparison of International and National Press Coverage of First Female Government Heads'. In: *Journalism Studies*, Vol. 9, No 3, 2008, pp. 429-446.

Caprioli, Mary. 'Gendered Conflict'. In: *Journal of Peace Research*, Vol. 37, No. 1, 2000, pp. 51-68.

Caprioli, Mary & Boyer, Mark A. 'Gender, Violence, and International Crisis'. In: *The Journal of Conflict Resolution*, Vol. 45, No. 4, 2001, pp. 503-518.

Carter Center. *Pre-Publication: Final Report National Elections in Liberia*. Atlanta, 2011. Available online at: http://www.cartercenter.org/resources/ pdfs/news/peace_publications/election_reports/liberia2011-finalrpt-pp.pdf (Accessed on 08 May 2012).

Central Intelligence Agency (CIA). *Liberia: Chiefs of State and Cabinet Members of Foreign Governments* [Website]. 2011. Available online at: https://www.cia.gov/library/publications/world-leaders-1/world-leaders-l/liberia.html (Accessed on 25 July 2011).

Central Intelligence Agency (CIA). *The World Factbook: Liberia* [Website]. 2011. Available online at: https://www.cia.gov/library/publications/the-world-factbook/geos/li.html (Accessed on 26 August 2011).

Cilliers, Jakkie & Mills, Greg (eds). *From Peacekeeping to Complex Emergencies: Peace Support Missions in Africa*. Johannesburg, South African Institute of International Affairs, 1999.

Cleaver, Gerry & Massey, Simon. 'Liberia: A Durable Peace at Last?' In: Furley, Oliver & May, Roy (eds.). *Ending Africa's Wars. Progressing to Peace*. Aldershot, Ashgate, 2006, pp. 179-199.

Cockburn, Cynthia. 'The Gendered Dynamics of Armed Conflict and Political Violence'. In: Moser, Caroline O. N. & Clark, Fiona C. (eds.) *Victims, Perpetrators or Actors? Gender, Armed Conflict and Political Violence*. London, Zed Books, 2001, pp. 13-29.

Cockburn, Cynthia. 'The Continuum of Violence: A Gender Perspective on War and Peace'. In: Giles, Wenona & Hyndman, Jennifer (eds.). *Sites of Violence: Gender and Conflict Zones*. London, University of California Press, 2004, pp. 24-44.

Cockburn, Cynthia. 'Militarism and War'. In: Shepherd, Laura J. (ed.). *Gender Matters in Global Politics: A Feminist Introduction to International Relations*. Abingdon, Routledge, 2010, pp. 105-115.

Cohn, Carol & Enloe, Cynthia. 'A Conversation with Cynthia Enloe: Feminists Look at Masculinity and the Men Who Wage War'. In: *Signs*, Vol. 28, No. 4, 2003, pp. 1187-1107.

Comprehensive Peace Agreement between the Government of Liberia and the Liberians United for Reconciliation and Democracy (LURD) and the Movement for Democracy in Liberia (MODEL) and Political Parties. 2003. Available online at: http://www.usip.org/files/file/resources/collections/peace_agreements/liberia_08182003.pdf (Accessed on 23 July 2011).

Conciliation Resources. *Accord Liberia Project* [Website]. 2011. Available online at: http://www.c-r.org/our-work/accord/liberia/index.php (Accessed on 08 July 2011).

Connell, Raewyn W. *Gender and Power: Society, the Person and Sexual Politics*. Cambridge, Polity Press, 1987.

Connell, Raewyn W. *The Men and the Boys.* Cambridge, Polity Press, 2000.

Connell, Raewyn W. *Gender.* Cambridge, Polity Press, 2002.

Connell, Raewyn W. *Masculinities.* Cambridge, Polity Press, 2005.

Constitution of the Republic of Liberia. 1986. Available online at: http://confinder.richmond.edu/admin/docs/liberia.pdf (Accessed on 21 July 2011).

Cook, Nikolas. *CRS Report for Congress: Liberia's Post-War Recovery: Key Issues and Developments*. Washington D.C., Congressional Research Service, 2007. Available online at: http://www.fas.org/sgp/crs/row/RL 33185.pdf (Accessed on 25 July 2011).

Cooper, Helene. 'Iron Lady: The Promise of Liberia's Ellen Johnson-Sirleaf'. In: *World Affairs*, November/December, 2010, pp. 41-50.

Cordel, Kristen. *Liberia: Women Peacekeepers and Human Security*. Open Democracy (8 October), 2009. Available online at: http://www. opendemocracy.net/blog/liberia/kristen-cordell/2009/10/08/liberia-women-peacekeepers-and-human-security (Accessed on 02 August 2011).

David, Charles-Philippe. 'Does Peacebuilding Build Peace? Liberal (Mis)steps in the Peace Process.' In: *Security Dialogue*, Vol. 30, No. 1, 1999.

Dennis, Peter. *A Brief History of Liberia*. New York, The International Center for Transitional Justice, 2006. Available online at: http://ictj.org/sites/ default/files/ICTJ-Liberia-Brief-History-2006-English.pdf (Accessed on 07 May 2012).

Department for International Development (DFID). *Conducting Conflict Assessments: Guidance Notes*. London, 2002. Available online at: http:// webarchive.nationalarhives.gov.uk/+/http://www.dfid.gov.uk/documents/ publications/conflictassessmentguidance.pdf (Accessed on 27 June 2011).

Derbyshire, Helen. *Gender Manual: A Practical Guide for Development Policy Makers and Practitioners*. London, Department for International Development, 2002. Available online at: http://www.allindiary.org/pool/ resources/dfid-gender-manual.pdf (Accessed on 11 May 2011).

Disney, Abigail E. & Reticker, Gini (dirs.). *Pray the Devil Back to Hell* [DVD Documentary]. New York, Fork Films, 2008.

Dittmer, Cordula. *Gender, Konflikt, Konfliktbearbeitung. Zivile und militärische Ansätze, Forderungen und Probleme*. Marburg (CCS Working Papers, No. 6), 2007, p. 4. Available online at: http://www.uni-marburg.de/ konfliktforschung/pdf/ccswp06 (Accessed on 28 April 2011).

Dwan, Renata & Bailey, Laura. *Liberia's Governance and Economic Management Assistance Programme (GEMAP): A joint review by the Department of Peacekeeping Operations' Peacekeeping Best Practices Section and the World Bank's Fragile States Group*. New York/Washington D.C., UN Department of Peacekeeping Operations/ The World Bank, 2006. Available online at: http://www.pbpu.unlb.org/ PBPS/Library/DPKO-WB%20joint%20review%20of%20GEMAP%20 FINAL.pdf (Accessed on 24 May 2012).

Ekiyor, Thelma Aremiebi & Gbowee, Leymah Roberta. *Women's Peace Activism in West Africa: The WIPNET Experience* [Website]. 2005. Available online at: http://www.peoplebuildingpeace.org/thestories/article.php?id=80&typ=theme&pid=18 (Accessed on 27 April 2011).

Economist. *Liberia's Feisty President: Another Round for Africa's Iron Lady: A Woman's Work Is Never Done* [Website]. 20 May, 2010. Available online at: http://www.economist.com/node/16168384 (Accessed on 04 May 2012).

El-Bushra, Judy. 'Transforming Conflict: Some Thoughts on a Gendered Understanding of Conflict Processes'. In: Jacobs, Susie, Jacobson, Ruth & Marchbank, Jennifer (eds.). *States of Conflict: Gender, Violence and Resistance*. London, Zed Books, 2000, pp. 66-86.

Elshtain, Jean Bethke. *Women and War*. Brighton, The Harvester Press, 1987.

Enloe, Cynthia. *Bananas, Beaches and Bases: Making Feminist Sense of International Politics*. Berkeley, University of California Press, 1989.

Ettang, Dorcas; Maina, Grace & Razia, Warigia. *A Regional Approach to Peacebuilding – The Mano River Region*. Durban, African Centre for the Constructive Resolution of Disputes (ACCORD), Policy and Practice Brief Issue 6 (May), 2011. Available online at: http://www.accord.org.za/downloads/brief/policy_practice6.pdf (Accessed on 17 August 2011).

Fischer Weltalmanach 2008. Frankfurt on the Main, Fischer Taschenbuch Verlag, 2007.

Fleshman, Michael. 'African Women Struggle for a Seat at the Peace Table'. In: *Africa Renewal* [Website], Vol. 16, No. 4, 2003. Available online at: http://www.un.org/ecosocdev/geninfo/afrec/vol16no4/164wm1.htm (Accessed on 25 April 2011).

Flood, Michael et al. (eds.). *International Encyclopedia of Men and Masculinities*. London, Routledge, 2007.

Francis, David J. *The Politics of Economic Regionalism: Sierra Leone in ECOWAS*. Aldershot, Ashgate, 2001.

Francis, David J. et al. *Dangers of Co-deployment: UN Co-operative Peacekeeping in Africa*. Aldershot, Ashgate, 2005.

Fuest, Veronika. "'This Is the Time to Get in Front': Changing Roles and Opportunities for Women in Liberia'. In: *African Affairs*, Vol. 107, No. 427, 2008, pp. 201–224.

Funder, Maria. 'Die Konflikttheorie feministischer Theorien'. In: Bonacker, Thorsten (ed.) *Sozialwissenschaftliche Konflikttheorien: Eine Einführung*. Wiesbaden, VS Verlag für Wissenschaften, 2008, pp. 293-318.

Furley, Oliver & May, Roy (eds.). *Ending Africa's Wars. Progressing to Peace*. Aldershot, Ashgate, 2006.

Galama, Anneke & Tongeren, Paul van (eds.). *Towards Better Peacebuilding Practice: On Lessons Learned, Evaluation Practices and Aid and Conflict*. Utrecht, European Centre for Conflict Prevention, 2003.

Galtung, Johan. 'An Editorial'. In: *Journal of Peace Research*, Vol. 1, No. 1, 1964, pp. 1-4.

'Gender and Peacebuilding'. Background Paper prepared for Working Group 12, organized by Cordaid and Pax Christi (the Netherlands) and International Alert (UK), for the International Conference *Towards Better Peacebuilding Practice*, October 24-26, 2001, Soesterberg, the Netherlands. In: Galama, Anneke & Tongeren, Paul van (eds.). *Towards Better Peacebuilding Practice: On Lessons Learned, Evaluation Practices and Aid and Conflict*. Utrecht, European Centre for Conflict Prevention, 2003, pp. 220-226.

George, Kla Emmanuel Gamoe. *Women as Agents of Peace During the Civil Wars in Liberia and Sierra Leone, 1989—2005*. Undated. (Mimeographed Paper). Available online at: www.isud.typepad.com/files/george1.doc (Accessed on 28 April 2011).

Gerdes, Felix. *Liberia* [Website]. Hamburg, Arbeitsgemeinschaft Kriegsursachenforschung, 2004. Available online at: http://www.sozialwiss.uni-hamburg.de/publish/Ipw/Akuf/kriege/260ak_liberia.htm (Accessed on 05 June 2011).

Gerring, John. *Case Study Research: Principles and Practices*. Cambridge, Cambridge University Press, 2007.

Gesellschaft für technische Zusammenarbeit (GTZ). *Towards Gender Mainstreaming in Crisis Prevention and Conflict Management: Guidelines for the German Technical Cooperation*. Eschborn, 2001.

Gesellschaft für technische Zusammenarbeit (GTZ). *Conflict Analysis for Project Planning and Management: A Practical Guideline - Draft*. Eschborn, 2001. Available online at: http://www.gtz.de/de/dokumente/en-crisis-conflictanalysis-2001.pdf (Accessed on 27 June 2011).

Ghana Center for Democratic Development. *Liberian Women's Initiative, LWI – Liberia (local)* [Website]. 2011. Available online at: http://www.cddghana.org/ngod.asp?ng=44htm (Accessed on 06 July 2011).

Gierycz, Dorota. 'Women, Peace and the United Nations: Beyond Beijing'. In: Skjelsbæk, Inger & Smith, Dan (eds.). *Gender, Peace and Conflict*. Oslo, International Peace Research Institute, 2001, pp. 14-31.

Giles, Wenona & Hyndman, Jennifer. 'Introduction: Gender and Conflict in a Global Context'. In: ibid. (eds.). *Sites of Violence: Gender and Conflict Zones*. London, University of California Press, 2004, pp. 3-23.

Giles, Wenona & Hyndman, Jennifer (eds.). *Sites of Violence: Gender and Conflict Zones*. London, University of California Press, 2004.

Global Security. *Liberia - Election and Coup Attempt – 1985* [Website]. Undated. Available online at: http://www.globalsecurity.org/military/world/war/liberia-1985.htm (Accessed on 28 August 2011).

Global Network of Women Peacebuilders (GNWP). *WIPNET* [Website]. Available online at: http://www.gnwp.org/members/wipnet (Accessed on 19 July 2011).

Goldstein, Joshua S. *War and Gender*. Cambridge, Cambridge University Press, 2001.

Governance Commission of Liberia. *Beyond Numbers: An Assessment of the Liberian Civil Society: A Report on the CIVICUS Civil Society Index 2010*. 2011. Available online at: http://www.civicus.org/images/stories/csi/csi_phase2/Liberia_ACR_final.pdf (Accessed on 26 July 2011).

Government of Liberia. *150 Day Action Plan: A Working Document for a New Liberia*. Undated. Available online at: http://allafrica.com/peaceafrica/resources/view/00010785.pdf (Accessed on 25 July 2011).

Government of Liberia, United Nations Liberia. *Factsheet: Empowering Women in Liberia: Joint Programme on Gender Equality and Women's Empowerment*. Undated. Available online at: http://www.unliberia.org/doc/genderemail.pdf (Accessed on 17 August 2011).

Great Initiative. *Liberia – Women Bringing Peace to the Country* [Website]. 2011. Available online at: http://www.thegreatinitiative.com/inspiring-story/liberia-mother-brownell/ (Accessed on 06 July 2011).

Grewal, Baljit Singh. *Johan Galtung: Positive and Negative Peace*. Auckland, 2003. Available online at: http://www.activeforpeace.org/no/fred/Positive_Negative_Peace.pdf (Accessed on 15 June 2011).

Hack, Nadine B. 'Liberia: Women's Mass Action For Peace and 'Pray the Devil Back to Hell' Screening at Samuel K Doe Stadium'. In: *AllAfrica*. 9 March, 2009. Available online at: http://allafrica.com/stories/200903 170823.html (Accessed on 08 July 2011).

Hamber, Brandon. 'Masculinity and Transitional Justice: An Exploratory Essay'. In: *The International Journal of Transitional Justice*, Vol. 1, 2007, pp. 375–390.

Harders, Cilja. 'Krieg und Frieden in internationalen Beziehungen'. In: Rosenberger, Sieglinde & Sauer, Birgit (eds.). *Politikwissenschaft und Geschlecht. Konzepte – Verknüpfungen – Perspektiven*. Wien, Facultas Verlag, 2004, pp. 229-249.

Harders, Cilja & Roß, Bettina (eds.). *Geschlechterverhältnisse in Krieg und Frieden: Perspektiven der feministischen Analyse internationaler Beziehungen*. Opladen, Leske & Budrich, 2002.

Harris, David. 'Liberia 2005: an Unusual African Post-conflict Election'. In: *Journal of Modern African Studies*, Vol. 44, No. 3, 2006, pp. 375–395.

Hayner, Priscilla B. *Unspeakable Truths: Transitional Justice and the Challenge of Truth Commissions*. Abingdon, Routledge, 2011.

Hearn, Jeff. 'Masculinity/Masculinities'. In: Flood, Michael et al. (eds.) *International Encyclopedia of Men and Masculinities*. London, Routledge, 2007, pp. 390-394.

Hearn, Jeff. 'Violence, Organisational and Collective'.In: Flood, Michael et al. (eds.) *International Encyclopedia of Men and Masculinities*. London, Routledge, 2007, pp. 618-621.

Higate, Paul. 'Military Institutions'. In: Flood, Michael et al. (eds.) *International Encyclopedia of Men and Masculinities*. London, Routledge, 2007, p. 441.

Howe, Herbert. 'Lessons from Liberia: ECOMOG and Regional Peacekeeping'. In: *International Security*, Vol. 21, No. 3, 1996, pp.145-176.

Hunt, Swanee & Posa, Christina. 'Women Waging Peace: Inclusive Security'. In: *Foreign Policy*, May/June, 2001, pp. 38-47.

Hutchings, Kimberley, 'Making Sense of Masculinity and War'. In: *Men and Masculinities*, Vol. 10, No. 4, 2008, pp. 389-404.

Integrated Regional Information Networks (IRIN). Liberia: Johnson Sirleaf Rejoins the Political Fray [Website]. 30 January, 2004. Available online at: http://www.irinnews.org/Report/48367/LIBERIA-Johnson-Sirleaf-rejoins-the-political-fray (Accessed on 20 April 2012).

Integrated Regional Information Networks (IRIN). *Liberia: "Humbled" Ellen Johnson-Sirleaf Confirmed Africa's First Female President* [Website]. 23 November, 2005. Available online at: http://www.irinnews.org/Report/57300/LIBERIA-Humbled-Ellen-Johnson-Sirleaf-confirmed-Africa-s-first-female-president (Accessed on 07 May 2012).

Integrated Regional Information Networks (IRIN). *Liberia: Opinion Divided on Truth and Reconciliation Findings* [Website]. 06 July, 2009. Available online at: http://www.irinnews.org/Report/85158/LIBERIA-Opinion-divided-on-Truth-and-Reconciliation-findings (Accessed on 10 May 2012).

Integrated Regional Information Networks (IRIN). *Liberia: TRC Furore Overshadows Peace Building Proposals* [Website]. 09 July, 2009. Available online at: http://www.irinnews.org/Report/85215/LIBERIA-TRC-furore-overshadows-peace-building-proposals (Accessed on 10 May 2012).

Integrated Regional Information Networks (IRIN). *Analysis: Do Liberians Know What They're Voting for?* [Website]. 05 August, 2011. Available online at: http://www.irinnews.org/Report/93431/Analysis-Do-Liberians-know-what-they-re-voting-for (Accessed on 10 May 2012).

International Crisis Group (ICG). *Liberia: Uneven Progress in Security Sector Reform.* Africa Report No. 148, 2009. Available online at: http://www.crisisgroup.org/en/regions/africa/west-africa/liberia/148-liberia-uneven-progress-in-security-sector-reform.aspx (Accessed on 20 July 2011).

International Crisis Group (ICG). Liberia: *How Sustainable is the Recovery?* Africa Report No. 177, 2011. Available online at: http://www.crisisgroup.

org/~/media/Files/africa/west-africa/liberia/177%20Liberia%20-20How%20Sustainable%20is%20the%20Recovery.pdf (Accessed on 02 May 2012).

Inter-Parliamentary Union (IPU). *Women in National Parliaments* [Website]. 2011. Available online at: http://www.ipu.org/wmn-e/world.htm (Accessed on 04 May 2012).

Jacobs, Susie, Jacobson, Ruth & Marchbank, Jennifer (eds.). *States of Conflict: Gender, Violence and Resistance*. London, Zed Books, 2000.

Jackson, Richard. 'Africa's Wars: Overview, Causes and the Challenges of Conflict Transformation'. In: Furley, Oliver & May, Roy (eds.). *Ending Africa's Wars. Progressing to Peace*. Aldershot, Ashgate, 2006, pp. 15-29.

Jalalzai, Farida & Krook, Mona Lena. 'Beyond Hillary and Benazir: Women's Political Leadership Worldwide'. In: *International Political Science Review*, Vol. 31, No. 1, 2010, pp. 5-21.

Jaye, Thomas. *Research Brief: Transitional Justice and DDR: The Case of Liberia*. New York, International Center for Transitional Justice, 2009. Available online at: http://ictj.org/sites/default/files/ICTJ-DDR-Liberia-ResearchBrief-2009-English_0.pdf (Accessed on 27 May 2012).

Jaye, Thomas. *Transitional Justice and DDR: The Case of Liberia*. New York, International Center for Transitional Justice, 2009. Available online at: http://ictj.org/sites/default/files/ICTJ-DDR-Liberia-CaseStudy-2009-English.pdf (Accessed on 25 May 2012).

Johnson-Sirleaf, Ellen. *Inaugural Address (16 January 2006)*. 2006. Available online at: http://www.emansion.gov.lr/doc/inaugural_add_1.pdf (Accessed on 25 July 2011).

Johnson-Sirleaf, Ellen. *Mein Leben für Liberia: Die erste Präsidentin Afrikas erzählt*. Frankfurt on the Main, Krüger Verlag, 2009.

Jones, Adam. 'Does 'Gender' Make the World Go Round? Feminist Critiques of International Relations'. In: *Review of International Studies*, No. 22, 1996, pp. 405-429.

Jones, Katelyn. 'West African Women Unite: The Inclusion of Women in Peace Processes'. In: *Undergraduate Transitional Justice Review*, Vol. 1, No. 2, 2011, pp. 156-172.

Jones-Demen, Annie. 'Dynamics of Gender Relations in War-time and Post-war Liberia: Implications for Public Policy'. In: Omeje, Kenneth (ed.). *War to Peace Transition: Conflict Intervention and Peacebuilding in Liberia*. Lanham, University Press of America, 2009, pp. 99-119.

Keating, Tom & Knight, W. Andy (eds.). *Building Sustainable Peace*. Edmonton, University of Alberta Press, 2004.

Kellow, Tim. *Women, Elections and Violence in West Africa: Assessing Women's Political Participation in Liberia and Sierra Leone*. London, International Alert, 2010. Available online at: http://www.international-alert.org/sites/default/files/publications/201012WomenElectionsViolence WestAfrica.pdf (Accessed on 20 July 2011).

Klotz, Audie, 'Case Selection'. In: Klotz, Audie & Prakash, Deepa (eds.). *Qualitative Methods in International Relations: A Pluralist Guide*. Basingstoke, Palgrave Macmillan, 2009, pp. 43-58.

Klotz, Audie, Prakash & Deepa (eds.). *Qualitative Methods in International Relations: A Pluralist Guide*. Basingstoke, Palgrave Macmillan, 2009.

Krasno, Jean. *External Study: Public Opinion Survey of UNMIL's Work in Liberia*. New York, 2006. Available online at: http://pbpu.unlb.org /PBPS/Library/Liberia_POS_final_report_Mar_29.pdf (Accessed on 28 July 2011).

Kreile, Renate. 'Dame, Bube, König... – Das neue große Spiel um Afghanistan und der Gender-Faktor'. In: *Leviathan*, Vol. 30, No. 1, 2002, pp. 34-64.

Kumar, Krishna. 'Civil Wars, Women and Gender Relations: An Overview'. In: ibid. (ed.). *Women and Civil War: Impact, Organizations and Action*. Boulder, Lynne Rienner, 2001, pp. 5-26.

Kumar, Krishna (ed.). *Women and Civil War: Impact, Organizations and Action*. Boulder, Lynne Rienner.

Landman, Todd. *Issues and Methods in Comparative Politics: An Introduction*. London, Routledge, 2003.

Large, Judith. 'Disintegration Conflicts and the Restructuring of Masculinity'. In: *Gender and Development*, Vol. 5, No. 2, 1997, pp. 23-30.

Mano River Union Women Peace Network (MARWOPNET). *MARWOPNET Liberia Country Report: December 2001-December 2003.* Undated. Available online at: http://www.marwopnet.org/liberia_activies.pdf (Accessed on 09 July 2011).

May, Larry et al. (eds.). *Rethinking Masculinity: Philosophical Explorations in Light of Feminism.* London, Rowman & Littlefield, 1996.

Mehler, Andreas & Smith-Höhn, Judy. 'Liberia: Ellen in Wonderland?' In: *GIGA Fokus,* No. 5, 2006. Available online at: http://www.gigahamburg.de/dl/download.php?d=/content/publikationen/pdf/gf_afrika_0605.pdf (Accessed on 20 July 2011).

Meintjes, Sheila. 'War and Post-War Shifts in Gender Relations'. In: Meintjes, Sheila; Pillay, Anu & Turshen, Meredeth (eds.). *The Aftermath: Women in Post-Conflict Transformation.* London, Zed Books, 2001, pp. 63-77.

Meintjes, Sheila; Pillay, Anu & Turshen, Meredeth (eds.). *The Aftermath: Women in Post-Conflict Transformation.* London, Zed Books, 2001.

Meyers Lexikonredaktion (eds.) *Meyers Neues Lexikon: In zehn Bänden: 7. Band: N-Pra.* Mannheim, Meyers Lexikonverlag, 1993.

Mordt, Gabriele. 'Das Geschlechterarrangement der klassischen Sicherheitspolitik'. In: Harders, Cilja & Roß, Bettina (eds.). *Geschlechterverhältnisse in Krieg und Frieden: Perspektiven der feministischen Analyse internationaler Beziehungen.* Opladen, Leske & Budrich, 2002, pp. 61-78.

Morrel, Robert & Ouzgane, Lahoucine. 'African Masculinities: An Introduction'. In: Ouzgane, Lahoucine & Morrel, Robert (eds.). *African Masculinities: Men in Africa from the Late Nineteenth Century to the Present.* Basingstoke, Palgrave Macmillan, 2005, pp. 1-19.

Moser, Caroline O. N. & Clark, Fiona C. 'Introduction'. In: ibid. (eds.). *Victims, Perpetrators or Actors? Gender, Armed Conflict and Political Violence.* London, Zed Books, 2001, pp. 3-12.

Moser, Caroline O. N. & Clark, Fiona C. (eds.) *Victims, Perpetrators or Actors? Gender, Armed Conflict and Political Violence.* London, Zed Books, 2001.

National Elections Commission (NEC). *2005 Elections Results: Results by Political Party and Gender* [Website]. 2005. Available online at:

http://www.necliberia.org/results/Senate/SenateByPPGender.html (Accessed on 30 August 2011).

National Elections Commission (NEC). *2005 Elections Results: Results by Political Party and Gender* [Website]. 2005. Available online at: http://www.necliberia.org/results/House/HouseByPPGender.html (Accessed on 30 August 2011).

Nilsson, Desirée & Söderberg Kovacs, Mimmi. 'Breaking the Cycle of Violence? Promises and Pitfalls of the Liberian Peace Process'. In: *Civil Wars*, Vol. 7, No. 4, 2005, pp. 396-414.

Nobel Prize. *The Nobel Peace Prize 2011: Ellen Johnson Sirleaf, Leymah Gbowee, Tawakkol Karman* [Website]. 2012. Available online at: http://www.nobelprize.org/nobel_prizes/peace/laureates/2011/johnson_sirleaf.html# (Accessed on 30 May 2012).

Nohlen, Dieter. 'Mikro-Makro-Analyse'. In: Nohlen, Dieter & Schultze, Rainer-Olaf (eds.). *Lexikon der Politikwissenschaft: Theorien, Methoden, Begriffe: Band 1 & 2*. München, Verlag C.H. Beck, 2004, p. 550.

Nohlen, Dieter & Schultze, Rainer-Olaf (eds.). *Lexikon der Politikwissenschaft: Theorien, Methoden, Begriffe: Band 1 & 2*. München, Verlag C.H. Beck, 2004.

Nordstrom, Carolyn. 'Visible Wars and Invisible Girls: Shadow Industries, and the Politics of Not-Knowing'. In: *International Feminist Journal of Politics*, No. 1, 1999, pp. 14-33.

Ogunsanya, Kemi. 'Qualifying Women's Leadership in Africa'. In: *Conflict Trends*, No. 2, 2007, pp. 50-54.

Omeje, Kenneth (ed.). *War to Peace Transition: Conflict Intervention and Peacebuilding in Liberia*. Lanham, University Press of America, 2009.

Organisation for Economic Co-operation and Development – Social Institutions and Gender Index (OECD-SIGI). *Gender Equality and Social Institutions in Liberia* [Website]. 2011. Available online at: http://www.genderindex.org/country/Liberia (Accessed on 21 July 2011).

Ouzgane, Lahoucine & Morrel, Robert (eds.). *African Masculinities: Men in Africa from the Late Nineteenth Century to the Present*. Basingstoke, Palgrave Macmillan, 2005.

Pankhurst, Donna. 'Introduction: Gendered War and Peace'. In: ibid. (ed.). *Gendered Peace: Women's Struggles for Post-War Justice and Reconciliation.* London, Routledge, 2008, pp. 1-30.

Pankhurst, Donna. 'Post-War Backlash Violence against Women: What Can "Masculinity" Explain?' In: ibid. (ed.). *Gendered Peace: Women's Struggles for Post-War Justice and Reconciliation.* London, Routledge, 2008, pp. 293-320.

Pankhurst, Donna (ed.). *Gendered Peace: Women's Struggles for Post-War Justice and Reconciliation.* London, Routledge, 2008.

Pankhurst, Donna. 'Sexual Violence in War'. In: Shepherd, Laura J. (ed.). *Gender Matters in Global Politics: A Feminist Introduction to International Relations.* Abingdon, Routledge, 2010, pp. 148-159.

Parpart, Jane L. & Zalewski, Marysia (eds.). *Rethinking the Man Question: Sex, Gender and Violence in International Relations.* London, Zed Books, 2008.

Pattynama, Pamela. 'Strangers and Double Self-consciousness: Feminism and Black Studies'. In: Buikema, Rosemarie & Smelik, Anneke. *Women's Studies and Culture: A Feminist Introduction.* London, Zed Books, 1993, pp. 135-147.

Paul, James-Allen; Weah, Aaron & Goodfriend, Lizzy. *Beyond the Truth and Reconciliation Commission: Transitional Justice Options in Liberia.* New York, International Center for Transitional Justice, 2010. Available online at: https://ictj.org/sites/default/files/ICTJ-Liberia-Beyond-TRC-2010-English.pdf (Accessed on 27 May 2012).

Peacebuilding Portal. *Liberian Women's Initiative (LWI)* [Website]. 2011. Available online at: http://www.peacebuildingportal.org/index.asp?pgid=9&org=2827 (Accessed on 07 July 2011).

Pedersen, Jennifer. 'In the Rain and in the Sun: Women in Peacebuilding in Liberia'. International Studies Association Annual Convention on *Bridging Multiple Divides.* San Francisco, 26-29 March 2008. Available online at: http://www.allacademic.com//meta/p_mla_apa_research_citation/2/5/3/1/3/pages253135/p253135-1.php (Accessed on 25 April 2011).

Peters, B. Guy. *Comparative Politics. Theory and Methods.* London, Macmillan Press, 1998.

Pierson, Paul. 'Increasing Returns, Path Dependence, and the Study of Politics'. In: *The American Political Science Review*, Vol. 94, No. 2, 2000, pp. 251-267.

Pillay, Anu. 'Violence against Women in the Aftermath'. In: Meintjes, Sheila; Pillay, Anu & Turshen, Meredeth (eds.). *The Aftermath: Women in Post-Conflict Transformation*. London, Zed Books, 2001, pp. 35-45.

Pillay, Anu. 'Truth Seeking and Gender: The Liberian Experience'. In: *African Journal on Conflict Resolution*, Vol. 9, No. 2, 2009, pp. 91-99. Available online at: http://www.accord.org.za/downloads/ajcr/ajcr_2009_2.pdf? phpMyAdmin=ceeda2df659e6d3e35a63d69e93228f1 (Accessed on 19 July 2011).

Pitts, Michelle. 'Sub-Regional Solutions for African Conflict: The ECOMOG Experiment'. In: *The Journal of Conflict* Studies [Website], Vol. 19, No. 1, 1999. Available online at: http://journals.hil.unb.ca/index.php/JCS/ article/view/4379/5057 (Accessed on 18 June 2011).

Pringle, Keith. 'Violence'. In: Flood, Michael et al. (eds.) *International Encyclopedia of Men and Masculinities*. London, Routledge, 2007, pp. 612-616.

Puechguirbal, Nadine. 'Peacekeeping, Peacebuilding and Post-conflict Reconstruction'. In: Shepherd, Laura J. (ed.). *Gender Matters in Global Politics. A Feminist Introduction to International Relations*. Abingdon, Routledge, 2010, pp. 161-175.

Rahman, Najat. 'Patriarchy'. In: Flood, Michael et al. (eds.). *International Encyclopedia of Men and Masculinities*. London, Routledge, 2007, pp. 468-470.

Ramsbotham, Oliver; Woodhouse, Tom & Miall, Hugh. *Contemporary Conflict Resolution: The Prevention, Management and Transformation of Deadly Conflicts*. Cambridge, Polity Press, 2005.

Reisinger, Christian. 'A Framework for the Analysis of Post-conflict Situations: Liberia and Mozambique Reconsidered. In: *International Peacekeeping*, Vol. 16, No. 4, 2009, pp. 483-498.

Reno, Williams. 'Anti-corruption Efforts in Liberia: Are They Aimed at the Right Targets?'. In: *International Peacekeeping*, Vol. 15, No. 3, 2008, pp. 387–404.

Réseau des Femmes du Fleuve Mano pour la Paix (REFMAP) [Website]. 2009. Available online at: http://www.marwopnet.org/index.html (Accessed on 09 July 2011).

Richards, Paul. 'Young Men and Gender in War and Postwar Reconstruction: Some Comparative Findings from Liberia and Sierra Leone. In: Bannon, Ian & Correia, Maria C. (eds.). *The Other Half of Gender: Men's Issues in Development.* Washington D.C., The World Bank, 2006, pp. 195-218.

Richmond, Oliver P. (ed.) *Palgrave Advances in Peacebuilding: Critical Developments and Approaches.* Basingstoke, Palgrave Macmillan, 2010.

Rosenberger, Sieglinde & Sauer, Birgit (eds.). *Politikwissenschaft und Geschlecht. Konzepte – Verknüpfungen – Perspektiven.* Wien, Facultas Verlag, 2004.

Sawyer, Amos. 'Emerging Patterns in Liberia's Post-Conflict Politics: Observations from the 2005 Elections'. In: *African Affairs*, Vol. 107, No. 427, 2008, pp. 177-199.

Schraeder, Peter J. *African Politics and Society: A Mosaic in Transformation.* Belmont, Wadsworth, 2004.

Schultze, Rainer-Olaf. 'Mehrebenen-Analyse'. In: Nohlen, Dieter & Schultze, Rainer-Olaf (eds.). *Lexikon der Politikwissenschaft: Theorien, Methoden, Begriffe: Band 1 & 2.* München, Verlag C.H. Beck, 2004, p. 528.

Schultze, Rainer-Olaf. 'Pfadabhängigkeit'. In: Nohlen, Dieter & Schultze, Rainer-Olaf (eds.). *Lexikon der Politikwissenschaft: Theorien, Methoden, Begriffe: Band 1 & 2.* München, Verlag C.H. Beck, 2004, pp. 683-384.

Seidler, Victor. 'Masculinity and Violence'. In: May, Larry et al. (eds.). *Rethinking Masculinity: Philosophical Explorations in Light of Feminism.* London, Rowman & Littlefield, 1996, pp. 63-75.

Shepherd, Laura J. 'Glossary'. In: ibid. (ed.). *Gender Matters in Global Politics. A Feminist Introduction to International Relations.* Abingdon, Routledge, 2010, pp. xix-xxv.

Shepherd, Laura J. 'Sex or Gender? Bodies in World Politics and Why Gender Matters'. In: ibid. (ed.). *Gender Matters in Global Politics. A Feminist Introduction to International Relations.* Abingdon, Routledge, 2010, pp. 3-16.

Shepherd, Laura J. (ed.). *Gender Matters in Global Politics. A Feminist Intro-duction to International Relations.* Abingdon, Routledge, 2010.

Skjelsbæk, Inger & Smith, Dan (eds.). *Gender, Peace and Conflict.* Oslo, International Peace Research Institute, 2001.

Solomon, Christiana. 'The Mano River Union Sub-region: The Role of Women in Building Peace'. In: Baksh, Rawwida et al. (eds.). *Gender Mainstreaming in Conflict Transformation: Building Sustainable Peace.* London, Commonwealth Secretariat, 2005, pp. 171-180.

Steans, Jill. *Gender and International Relations: An Introduction.* Cambridge, Polity Press, 1998.

Svensson, Katja. 'Women Hold up Half the Sky: Peace and Security Lessons from Liberia'. In: *African Security Review*, Vol. 17, No. 4, 2008, pp. 178-183.

Sweetman, Caroline (ed.). *Gender, Peacebuilding and Reconstruction.* Oxford, Oxfam GB, 2005.

Thomas, Gwynn & Adams, Melinda. 'Breaking the Final Glass Ceiling: The Influence of Gender in the Elections of Ellen Johnson-Sirleaf and Michelle Bachelet'. In: *Journal of Women*, Vol. 31, No. 2, 2010, pp. 105-131.

Time. *Top Female Leaders around the World* [Website]. 2012. Available online at: http://www.time.com/time/specials/packages/article/0,28804, 2005455_2005458_2005482,00.html (Accessed on 04 May 2012).

Tonpo, Jarlawah. 'Johnson Sirleaf: 'Taylor Fooled Me''. In: *New African*, May 2009, pp. 40-43.

Transparency International. *Corruption by Country/Territory* [Website]. 2011. Available online at: http://www.transparency.org/country#LBR_Data Research_SurveysIndices (Accessed on 24 May 2012).

Truth and Reconciliation Commission of Liberia. *"Inheritance Law Not Pro-tecting Women"... Attorney Deweh Gray* [Website]. Press Releases. Undated. Available online at: http://trcofliberia.org/press_releases/109 (Accessed on 21 July 2011).

Truth and Reconciliation Commission. *Volume II: Consolidated Final Report.* Monrovia, 2009, p. 361. Available online at: http://trcofliberia.org/

resources/reports/final/volume-two_layout-1.pdf (Accessed on 20 April 2012).

Turshen, Meredeth & Twagiramariya, Clotilde (eds.). *What Women Do in Wartime: Gender and Conflict in Africa.* London, Zed Books, 1998.

United Nations (UN). *Charter of the United Nations and Statute of the International Court of Justice.* San Francisco, 1945. Available online at: http://treaties.un.org/doc/Publication/CTC/uncharter.pdf (Accessed on 18 August 2011).

United Nations (UN). *United Nations Prize in the Field of Human Rights: 2003 Awardees* [Website]. Undated. Available online at: http://www.un.org/events/humanrights/2003/awards.html (Accessed on 09 July 2011).

United Nations (UN). *Liberia.* Undated. Available online at: http://www.un.org/Depts/Cartographic/map/profile/liberia.pdf (Accessed on 06 August 2011).

United Nations. *UNMIL: United Nations Mission in Liberia* [Website]. Undated. Available online at: http://www.un.org/en/peacekeeping/missions/unmil/mandate.shtml (Accessed on 18 August 2011).

United Nations Development Fund for Women (UNIFEM). *Securing the Peace: Guiding the International Community towards Women's Effective Participation throughout Peace Processes.* New York, 2005. Available online at: http://www.unifem.org/attachments/products/Securing_the_Peace.pdf (Accessed on 09 May 2011).

United Nations Development Fund for Women (UNIFEM). *Women's Participation in Peace Negotiations: Connections between Presence and Influence.* New York, 2009. Available online at: http://www.realizingrights.org/pdf/UNIFEM_handout_Women_in_peace_processes_Brief_April_2 0_2009.pdf (Accessed on 25 August 2011).

United Nations Development Programme (UNDP). *Liberia Annual Report 2009.* Monrovia, 2009. Available online at: http://www.lr.undp.org/Documents/RecentPublic/UNDP%20Liberia%20Annual%20Report%20 2009.pdf (Accessed on 18 June 2011).

United Nations Development Programme (UNDP). *Human Development Report 2010: The Real Wealth of Nations: Pathways to Human Development.* New York, 2010. Available online at: http://hdr.undp.org/en/reports/global/hdr2010/chapters/ (Accessed on 23 August 2012).

United Nations Development Programme (UNDP). *Liberia: Country Profile of Human Development Indicators* [Website]. New York, 2011. Available online at: http://hdrstats.undp.org/en/countries/profiles/LBR.html (Accessed on 18 June 2011).

United Nations Educational, Scientific and Cultural Organization (UNESCO) (ed.). *Women and Peace in Africa: Case Studies on Traditional Conflict Resolution Practices.* Paris, 2003. Available online at: http://unesdoc. unesco.org/images/0013/001332/133274e.pdf (Accessed on 02 May 2011).

United Nations General Assembly. *Liberia Is Writing New History for Its Women and Girls Delegation Tells Women's Anti-Discrimination Committee, Admitting Great Challenges in That Endeavour* [Website]. New York, 2009. Available online at: http://www.un.org/News/Press/docs/ 2009/wom1748.doc.htm (Accessed on 20 July 2011).

United Nations General Assembly. *Convention on the Elimination of All Forms of Discrimination against Women* [Website]. New York, 2011. Available online at: http://www.un.org/womenwatch/daw/cedaw/text/ econvention.htm (Accessed on 27 June 2011).

United Nations High Commissioner for Refugees (UNHCR). *2003 UNHCR Statistical Yearbook: Country Data Sheet – Liberia.* Geneva, 2005. Available online at: http://www.unhcr.org/41d2c182c.html (Accessed on 27 August 2011).

United Nations Security Council (UNSC). *Resolution 1325 (2000).* New York, 2000. Available online at: http://www.un.org/events/res_1325e.pdf (Accessed on 27 October 2010).

United Nations Security Council (UNSC). *Resolution 1497 (2003).* New York, 2003. Available online at: http://daccess-dds-ny.un.org/doc/UNDOC/ GEN/N03/449/48/PDF/N0344948.pdf?OpenElement (Accessed on 19 July 2011).

United Nations Security Council (UNSC). *Resolution 1509 (2003).* New York, 2003. Available online at: http://www.un.org/ga/search/view_doc.asp? symbol=S/RES/1509%282003%29 (Accessed on 19 July 2011).

United Nations Security Council (UNSC). *Resolution 1820 (2008).* New York, 2008. Available online at: http://daccess-dds-ny.un.org/doc/UNDOC/ GEN/N08/391/44/PDF/N0839144.pdf?OpenElement (Accessed on 25 August 2011).

United Nations Security Council (UNSC). *Resolution 2008 (2011)*. New York, 2011. Available online at: http://www.un.org/ga/search/view_doc.asp? symbol=S/RES/2008%282011%29 (Accessed on 25 May 2012).

United Nations Women. *Beijing and its Follow-up* [Website]. 2011. Available online at: http://www.un.org/womenwatch/daw/followup/beijing+5.htm (Accessed on 22 April 2011).

United Nations Women. *Women, War and Peace* [Website]. Undated. Available online at: http://www.womenwarpeace.org/ (Accessed on 25 August 2011).

United States Agency for International Development (USAID). *Gender Terminology*. Undated. Available online at: http://www.usaid.gov/our_work/ cross-cutting_programs/wid/pubs/Gender_Terminology_2.pdf (Accessed on 18 August 2011).

United States Agency for International Development (USAID). *Liberia: Country Profile*. Undated. Available online at: http://www.usaid.gov/locations/ sub-saharan_africa/countries/liberia/liberia_profile.pdf (Accessed on 18 June 2011).

U.S. Department of State. *Background Note: Liberia* [Website]. 2011. Available online at: http://www.state.gov/r/pa/ei/bgn/6618.htm#history (Accessed on 27 August 2011).

Vann, Beth. *Gender-Based Violence: Emerging Issues in Programs Serving Displaced Populations*. Arlington, Reproductive Health for Refugees Consortium, 2002. Available online at: http://reliefweb.int/sites/reliefweb. int/files/resources/DA3C3605C463011DC1256D2D005A99E2-rhrc-BV-jan03.pdf (Accessed on 29 August 2011).

Väyrynen, Tarja. 'Gender and Peacebuilding'. In: Richmond, Oliver P. (ed.) *Palgrave Advances in Peacebuilding: Critical Developments and Approaches*. Basingstoke, Palgrave Macmillan, 2010, pp. 137-153.

Waylen, Georgina. *Gender in Third World Politics*. Buckingham, Open University Press, 1996.

West Africa Network for Peacebuilding (WANEP). *Rapport Annuel 2009*. Accra, WANEP, 2009. Available online at: http://www.wanep.org/wanep/ attachments/article/202/ar_2009_fr.pdf (Accessed on 20 August 2011).

Whitehead, Stephen M. 'Patriarchal Dividend'. In: Flood, Michael et al. (eds.) *International Encyclopedia of Men and Masculinities*. London, Routledge, 2007, pp. 467-468.

'Women of Liberia's Mass Action for Peace'. In: *The Scavenger: Salvaging What's Left after the Masses Have Had Their Feed*. Undated. Available online at: http://www.thescavenger.net/people/women-of-liberias-mass-action-for-peace-37462-315.html (Accessed on 07 June 2012).

Women World Leaders 1945-2011 [Website]. 2011. Available online at: http://www.terra.es/personal2/monolith/00women.htm (Accessed on 07 May 2012).

World Bank. *Data and Statistics* [Website]. 2011. Available online at: http://web.worldbank.org/WBSITE/EXTERNAL/COUNTRIES/AFRICAE XT/LIBERIAEXTN/0,,menuPK:356220~pagePK:141132~piPK:141109~t heSitePK:356194,00.html (Accessed on 27 August 2011).

Wrong, Michela. 'World View - Michela Wrong Doubts If a Woman Is Any Better'. In: *New Statesman,* 28 November, 2005. Available online at: http://www.newstatesman.com/node/152092 (Accessed on 09 May 2012).

Yacob-Haliso, Olajumoke. 'If I Could Speak to Madam President: Returnee Women's Experiences of Return, Reintegration and Peace in Liberia'. In: *Liberian Studies Journal*, Vol. 33, No. 1, 2008, pp. 1-22.

Zalewski, Marysia. 'Feminist International Relations: Making Sense...' In: Shepherd, Laura J. (ed.). *Gender Matters in Global Politics. A Feminist Introduction to International Relations*. Abingdon, Routledge, 2010, pp. 28-43.

Zalewski, Marysia & Parpart, Jane L. 'Introduction: Rethinking the Man Question'. In: Parpart, Jane L. & Zalewski, Marysia (eds.). *Rethinking the Man Question: Sex, Gender and Violence in International Relations*. London, Zed Books, 2008, pp. 1-22.

Zanzibar Declaration: Women of Africa for a Culture of Peace [Website]. 1999. Available online at: http://www.unesco.org/cpp/uk/declarations/ zanzibar.htm (Accessed on 02 May 2011).

Zuckerman, Elaine & Greenberg, Marcia. 'The Gender Dimensions of Post-Conflict Reconstruction: An Analytical Framework for Policymakers'. In:

Sweetman, Caroline (ed.). *Gender, Peacebuilding and Reconstruction*. Oxford, Oxfam GB, 2005, pp. 70-82.

ibidem-Verlag / *ibidem* Press
Melchiorstr. 15
70439 Stuttgart
Germany

ibidem@ibidem.eu
www.ibidem-verlag.com
www.ibidem.eu

CPSIA information can be obtained
at www.ICGtesting.com
Printed in the USA
LVOW13s2134160117
521174LV00012B/968/P